HOW DOES IT FEEL
TO BE UNWANTED?

HOW DOES IT FEEL TO BE UNWANTED?

STORIES OF RESISTANCE AND RESILIENCE FROM MEXICANS LIVING IN THE UNITED STATES

EILEEN TRUAX

TRANSLATED BY DIANE STOCKWELL

BEACON PRESS
BOSTON

BEACON PRESS
Boston, Massachusetts
www.beacon.org

Beacon Press books
are published under the auspices of
the Unitarian Universalist Association of Congregations.

21 20 19 18   8 7 6 5 4 3 2 1

This book is printed on acid-free paper that meets the uncoated paper
ANSI/NISO specifications for permanence as revised in 1992.

Text design and composition by Kim Arney
Translated by Diane Stockwell

Lyrics of Los Jornaleros del Norte reprinted here with
permission of Omar León.

Library of Congress Cataloging-in-Publication Data

Names: Truax, Eileen, author.
Title: How does it feel to be unwanted? : stories of resistance and resilience
    from Mexicans living in the United States / Eileen Truax.
Description: Boston : Beacon Press, 2018. | Includes bibliographical references.
Identifiers: LCCN 2018005022 (print) | LCCN 2018018254 (ebook) |
    ISBN 9780807073414 (e-book) | ISBN 9780807073384 (paperback)
Subjects: LCSH: Mexicans—United States. | Immigrants—United States. |
    Discrimination—United States. | United States—Emigration and
    immigration—Social aspects. | Mexico—Emigration and immigration—Social
    aspects. | BISAC: SOCIAL SCIENCE / Emigration & Immigration. | SOCIAL
    SCIENCE / Discrimination & Race Relations. | SOCIAL SCIENCE / Ethnic
    Studies / Hispanic American Studies.
Classification: LCC E184.M5 (ebook) | LCC E184.M5 T78 2018 (print) |
    DDC 973/.046872—dc23
LC record available at https://lccn.loc.gov/2018005022

To my son, Guillermo,
for his endless light.

CONTENTS

THIRTY YEARS OF RESISTANCE

THE IDEA FOR THIS BOOK emerged a few days after Donald Trump's presidential victory in November 2016. Because of my experience writing about immigrant communities, people started asking me how Mexicans in the US would defend themselves now that he was president and after he had attacked them so viciously. And every time I attempted to reply, I came up with the same answer: the "defense" has already been mounted; it will just be put into action once again. What I meant is that the immigrant communities that came under attack during Trump's campaign—and presidency—have been targeted and beaten down for decades and via a succession of presidents, both Republican and Democrat. And, like all minorities in this country—religious, racial, and ethnic—in order to triumph, Mexicans in the United States have first had to resist.

This book recounts the stories of men and women who left Mexico ten, twenty, or thirty years ago in search of a better life in the United States. They have faced violations of their rights and their dignity and have suffered all manner of violence. Like millions, these Mexican men and women have worked diligently over the course of three decades to create networks of resistance and solidarity and keep forging ahead. They have refused to be the victims of the broken systems of both countries and have triumphed over adversity against all expectations. Thanks to this history of struggle and perseverance, on both sides of the border, they are standing up to the politicians in the United States who convey, in words and in actions, that they are not wanted here.

For those of us who have lived in the US for decades, racism, xenophobia, and classism are mainstays of the social fabric, just like many other aspects of a nation's complex identity. I have lived in this country for fourteen years, working as a journalist all the while, immersed in the issue of immigration. I have written two other books and dozens of articles, and I've read hundreds more on this subject. But for many people, the prejudice and xenophobia only became noticeable when Donald Trump arrived on the scene, as his rise often became the shorthand explanation for the ills of society. One day after the election, denunciations of racist and anti-immigrant attacks began to appear from across the country, which, thanks to the magic of "share" and "retweet" buttons, pointed to a seeming escalation of hate crimes. But escalation as compared to what, if most people don't know what the previous figures were that might prove an increase?

Certainly, Trump's campaign rhetoric and the insults and threats he has hurled once in office have meant that those who hold racist and anti-immigrant views now feel validated, with a greater right to openly question, attack, and incite violence against minorities. Events such as the clash in Charlottesville, Virginia, in August 2017, when a rally of white supremacists ended in the death of one counterprotester and injuries to several others, have fueled this perception. But the history of racism and xenophobia in the United States goes back centuries, and it has survived, and in some instances even sharpened, in recent decades. White supremacist ideologies and proposals to limit the exercise of civil rights are a latent virus that boldly resurfaces under certain circumstances. Personalities such as Donald Trump should not be viewed as a cause but as a consequence. The atmosphere in the United States in recent years is a symptom of a social dynamic that follows the pendulum theory: for every advance by progressive groups, there's a simultaneous reaction in the opposite direction.

In August 2014, the Southern Poverty Law Center published its report on hate groups in the United States; there were 939. That's almost a thousand hate groups, including neo-Nazis, the KKK, skinhead racists, white nationalists, anti-LGBT groups, anti-

Muslim groups, black separatists, border vigilantes, and other anti-immigrant groups. Of those, half were located in the South. In the four states bordering Mexico alone—California, Arizona, New Mexico, and Texas—there are 160 active hate groups. There has been a pronounced uptick especially in California and Arizona, where the predominant groups are anti-immigrant and anti-Latino.[1]

Between 2000 and 2013, the number of hate groups in the United States grew by 56 percent. This period coincided with a reinforcement of border security in the wake of the terrorist attacks of September 11, 2001; an increase in the proportion of nonwhite immigrants; the financial recession of 2008–9; and the election of Barack Obama, the first African American president. All of these factors contributed to the growth of hate groups. And, yes, many of these elements were opportunistically exploited in Trump's campaign rhetoric. People who sympathized with the views of those groups found a spokesman who validated their outrage, but they were already in place before Trump came along. In a 2012 report, the FBI registered more than 5,000 hate crimes, involving over 7,000 victims. The number increased to 5,800 in 2015 and 6,100 in 2016. In those three years, more than half were targeted because of bias against the victim's race or ethnicity.[2]

With the prevalence of mobile devices and social media, these incidents can be easily and widely disseminated, and that in turn has opened the door to higher rates of prosecution and conviction for these crimes. The public's perception may be that the number and frequency of these incidents is rising, but data from past years would have to be carefully reviewed for comparison to confirm that.

The data plainly shows that racial violence and discrimination are a mundane daily reality among certain communities in the United States, particularly for Mexicans and Mexican Americans. All of us who were born outside the US or are the children of immigrants have heard at one time or another *"Go back to your country!"*—the first time for me was outside a supermarket in 2005. And we have all been the victims of or have witnessed some type of racial violence that has made us feel fearful and profoundly unwanted in this country we call home. None of this is Trump's fault: the incendiary rhetoric spewing from the White House is not the cause of this country's problems—or those of our neighbor to the south—but the result.

Chapter 2, for example, includes the story of Claudia Amaro, from Kansas, who inspired the title for this book. I have known Claudia for five years and have closely followed her and her family's continuing story. In one of our most recent conversations, Claudia told me that once when she was feeling particularly hopeless she had asked a white woman, "Why doesn't the US want us?" In my experience, this is the question that immigrants puzzle over, the question that gets under their skin, especially when they are the victims of workplace abuse or bigoted comments, when their children are victims of bullying at school, or when a politician in power insults and stigmatizes an entire community in spite of their struggle and hard work every day.

The thirteen stories presented in this book reflect the stories of the millions of Mexicans in the United States. Most of the protagonists in these pages arrived in this country undocumented; some have managed to attain legal status, while others are still fighting for it. Three of them came to the United States with legal documents but had to overcome obstacles stemming from language barriers or their country of origin, skin color, or sexual orientation. Some stories have to do with work done by the Mexican community in the US to defend civil and human rights: the right to health care, education, work with dignity, access to information, family reunification, political representation—and the right to live peacefully in the land where one works and, in spite of everything, the land one loves.

All thirteen stories are based on interviews conducted specifically for this book. The chapters also include anecdotes and excerpts from related stories I covered over the past thirteen years; some while I was a reporter for the Los Angeles daily *La Opinión*, and others as a contributor to the Mexican daily paper *El Universal*. I have included them to provide a broader context for the central stories and as a reminder that what some today see as an aberration is a continuation of thirty years of perseverance.

I hope this book will help readers feel more connected, that it will enable them to feel closer to those "others" who are a part of their community—the millions of Mexicans who, with their great strength and courage, help to power the engine of the US economy and who, with tremendous generosity, help alleviate the poverty of those they left behind. Through their stories, beyond the realm of politics, I hope we can see them as the essence of two countries that owe them a great debt and understand that they should be viewed as a valued—and wanted—people.

CHAPTER ONE

A BETTER LIFE

Omar León, forty
Atapaneo, Michoacán/Los Angeles, California

AT SEVEN IN THE MORNING, a dozen Latino men stand outside the entrance to the Home Depot on Sunset Boulevard, waiting for the first customers to arrive. A man parks his pickup and approaches the group. After a brief negotiation, three men drive off with him in the truck loaded up with construction materials. They have a job, at least for the day.

For those unfamiliar with the day-to-day reality for undocumented workers in the US, the scene looks like something out of a movie: *A Better Life*, to be specific, released in 2012 and directed by Chris Weitz. The film tells the story of Carlos Galindo, a day laborer played by the Mexican actor Demián Bichir, who was nominated for an Oscar for Best Actor for his performance.

But the life of Carlos Galindo, a groundskeeper whose fortunes hang by a tenuous thread because he lacks papers to work legally, is not the stuff of fiction. Every day across the country, around 120,000 day laborers gather outside Home Depots and other home improvement stores, in parking lots, at bus stops, searching for, in effect, a better life.

Omar León knows this life like few others do. Born in Michoacán state in Mexico, he arrived in the United States to join his family when he was eleven years old, and he quickly joined the day laborers' ranks. He worked doing odd jobs, painting, gardening, and in construction, until he decided to get involved in activism and started organizing other workers to fight for their rights. Now, he is the workforce development coordinator at the National Day Laborer Organizing Network (NDLON), which promotes leadership and defends the rights of working immigrants.

"Our migration isn't because of one thing; it's because of the crisis our country has been in for years, for decades." This cutting observation basically summarizes Omar's family history, much like that of hundreds of thousands of other Mexican families over the last several decades. His parents had settled in the small town of Atapaneo in Michoacán, had five children, and tried to raise them as best they could. When it became clear they could not adequately support their children on their meager earnings, they decided to come to the United States, even though they were undocumented. One of Omar's older brothers went first, followed by the others. Omar was the last to make the trip north, and the family was separated for two years. His brothers remember that his father desperately wanted Omar to join them as soon as possible. When the family sat down to dinner, their mother would cry, thinking about the son left behind. Finally, when Omar was eleven he set out on the journey north.

Omar crossed the border with a group, trekking over the mountains. "After that, a car picked us up, and that was the hardest part of the trip. We got into a small car, and they said it was going to be a very short drive. There were people in the trunk, women with four people piled over their feet. People sitting had their legs over us, and I felt like I couldn't breathe, that I wasn't going to make it. I couldn't feel my body anymore." Finally, they arrived at the house where they would wait for their families to pick them up.

His parents were accustomed to struggling, so when they got to the US, it was nothing new. Omar remembers several very hard years in Mexico, "not because they weren't hardworking, but because there were very few opportunities." If you're a person of limited means, he explains, you don't have many ways to get ahead. But his parents applied the same tireless work ethic they had exercised in Mexico to their new country. They settled in Santa Maria, a farming town in California's Central Valley, and started working in the fields. Omar's mother worked cleaning hotel rooms, and when her shift was over, she would walk along the beach nearby, collecting bottles and cans to redeem.

"My parents always made an extra effort," Omar said. "They set an example of doing everything you can to support your family. Soon after we got here, there was a legalization for people who worked in the fields, so our family got legal status in 1993."

Ever since he was a child, Omar has been interested in music. His mother noticed, but his family could not afford to buy him an instrument in Mexico. Once in the US, she saved up some of the extra money she made redeeming cans and bought Omar his first keyboard.

Music brought him to Los Angeles. One day, Omar saw a notice for a band audition, so he tried out and became a member. But having a musical instrument, and the talent to play it, is not enough to make it in the music business; you also need experience. No members of the band had any previous experience, and they signed a record contract that turned out to be less than favorable to them. They signed away all the rights to their music to the record company and ran into problems with their management. In the end, Omar found himself unemployed in Los Angeles.

He tried to earn money however he could. Walking around the city, he saw that day laborers would gather on some street corners, waiting for someone to come by and offer a job, talking among themselves to pass the time. "I started hanging around talking to them too, until one day, just from becoming friends with those guys and seeing me there so much, they hired me too."

Once Omar entered the day laborer world, he liked it: hardworking men who face a great deal of challenges, who put themselves out there and may have bad experiences, running the risk of not getting paid by the people who hire them. But at the same time, he discovered they were entrepreneurs, as he describes it. They manage their own schedules, they don't have a steady boss they have to report to, and they build their own support networks. He discovered those networks are established organizations that aim to protect workers from the potentially negative aspects of this kind of work.

Omar joined the Hollywood Community Job Center, one of four centers coordinated by the Instituto de Educación Popular del Sur de California (IDEPSCA), located just a few blocks away from a local Home Depot. These stores are popular spots for laborers to gather and be hired by anyone needing their services, from painting a wall, installing a floor, performing plumbing work, or installing electrical wiring.

Just twenty years old at the time, Omar was not skilled in any particular area, but the other workers liked him, and he spoke English. They brought him along as a helper, and that's how he got his start. When he started spending time at the job center, he found friendly leadership, coffee in the mornings, English classes, and a generally more organized system of working than out on the street corners. Day laborers who wanted to work would go by the center every day, and people in need of their services would hire them through the center.

"I liked their system. Out on the street corner, there's a little more risk, because some people don't like cars stopping in the street, even though they have the right to pull over by the curb. The workers get harassed sometimes, some guys drive by and throw trash at you, so you always have to be on your guard. Once, somebody threw a cup of hot McDonald's coffee at a worker. Sometimes somebody will stop, you think maybe they're going to hire you, but they spit at you. At the center, everything's more organized. The hirer comes in, a staffer works with him, and he chooses the workers."

When Omar began working at the center in 2002, he also got involved as a volunteer, organizing the workers. He woke up eager to go there. He didn't always get work, but he enjoyed the camaraderie of spending time with other people like him. They started to feel like his family. He also started learning more about what was going on in politics and in the labor movement, at the local, state, and national levels. Omar worked at the center for a few years and got involved in organizing the day labor movement. He wound up serving as coordinator for the day laborer program of IDEPSCA and worked there for eight years.

"It was a great life experience for me, really beautiful, because a day laborer became a manager for the national day-laborer project, coordinating several different centers. We could implement things at the organizational level. And that's where I met Pablo Alvarado."

Pablo Alvarado was born into a family of poor rural farmers in El Salvador. As a child, he worked in the fields to help support the family while also attending school. When Pablo was just ten years old, he volunteered to teach adults how to read. At the age of twelve, with the civil war raging, he became an assistant literature teacher. He eventually earned his teaching credentials, but the necessity of migrating to the US meant he had to start over from nothing. He worked as a gardener, driver, painter, and builder. And just like Omar, over the years, Pablo became increasingly involved in political work and organizing other workers. He is now the executive director of NDLON.

Pablo and Omar first met through their work with day laborers, but music is what drew them together. Although music had always been his passion, after his bad experience with the band in Los Angeles, Omar decided to have nothing more to do with it and to focus on organizing day laborers. But one evening, when he stayed later than usual at the IDEPSCA office, he heard music coming from the basement. A band was rehearsing. Hearing the notes from the keyboard and the percussion rhythms, Omar could not resist. He got up from his desk and went to the basement, where a little studio had been set up. The band was Los Jornaleros del Norte.

"I was stunned. They didn't know me as a musician; they knew me as the coordinator of centers for workers, but they invited me to sit in. And putting a musician in front of an instrument, you can't keep them from playing it, right?" he says with a laugh. "I went over to the piano and started to play."

Pablo was not at rehearsal that day, but his bandmates told him that Omar had talent. And even though Omar insisted he wanted nothing more to do with the music business, Pablo won him over. Los Jornaleros del Norte had a mission, and it wasn't about making money but about bringing happiness to everyone in the pro-immigrant, pro-labor movement. Omar agreed to go to a rehearsal.

Omar tells me what a lucky day that was for him. "We all had our jobs and obligations, but Los Jornaleros del Norte reconnected me with my true passion, music, in a very real, healthy way, totally separated from trying to make a hit or make a lot of money." Their goal was simply to inspire the movement through their songs, with simple, heartfelt lyrics. The band played at marches and protests, calling out bosses who refused to pay workers, robbing them of wages. "People really appreciate what we do, and it moves them and motivates them."

Adding Omar turned out to be one of the best decisions the band ever made. Aside from singing, playing piano and accordion, and having a great stage presence—with his dark hair combed back, warm eyes, and bright smile—Omar has written most of the lyrics to Los Jornaleros del Norte songs on three of the four albums they have released so far.

Yo solo quiero probar un pedacito de justicia
Yo solo quiero tomar solo un traguito de dignidad
Ya conocí la tristeza, el llanto, el odio, el racismo, pobreza, separo
Amargura, desprecio, maltrato, más nunca, más nunca la libertad.

I only want to taste a little justice
I only want a little sip of dignity
I have already had sadness, tears, hatred, racism, poverty, separation,
Bitterness, abuse, but never, never freedom.

"I consider myself a musician, but I'm not super talented," Omar tells me modestly. "I think I'm creative. The lyrics I write for the movement are heard at the marches, as slogans, they're stories we see or hear about, that I've been able to make into songs using simple melodies."

Ya me he tragado la explotación
Pues me ha robado mucho el patrón
Me he emborrachado de soledad
Con mi familia quisiera estar.

I have swallowed exploitation
Since the boss has robbed me so much
I have gotten drunk out of loneliness
I just wanted to be with my family.

The first time I heard Los Jornaleros del Norte was in Phoenix, Arizona, in late May 2010. It was a Saturday, and hot, hinting at the desert summer soon to arrive. Hundreds of thousands of people from all over the country marched through the streets to protest SB 1070, the anti-immigrant Arizona law that would go into effect at the end of July and would require police officers to stop and question any person who "looked" undocumented.

Of the many protests staged against the law, the "Alto Arizona!" campaign, organized by NDLON and the activist organization Puente, stood out because Los Jornaleros del Norte played at all the events. The band had all their equipment set up on a flatbed truck and used that as their stage, playing and singing, mixing catchy rhythms and hooks with lyrics about immigration raids and deportation, but also about hope.

That afternoon in May, Omar debuted a new song: "Racismo en Arizona," which became the anthem of the movement against the law in the coming months.

Pero la raza es fregona
se las sabe todititas
si nos sacan por la tarde
regresamos de mañanita.

But our people are stubborn
Everybody knows
If they kick us out in the evening
We'll be back the next morning.

It's easy to miss the way in. It's practically impossible to see from the highway, but it's right there: a slight gap in the brush and weeds that turns into a kind of tunnel leading down into a ravine. Continuing along the path from there, about fifteen minutes later, scrambling through ditches and following the twists and turns through the undergrowth, you come to a small grouping of makeshift dwellings. Patched together with sticks, scraps of rubber, cardboard, with whatever materials they could find, out in the woods, these handmade homes provide a place to spend the night.

Dozens and possibly hundreds of day workers live like this in the city of Vista, in northern San Diego County. They came there chasing a dream and work, if hired, constructing luxury homes. At the end of the long day, they retreat to their little shacks in the woods, hidden from immigration authorities.

La Jolla, one of the wealthiest communities per capita in the country, is also close by, with fabulous homes up in the hills with spectacular views of the Pacific Ocean. There are plenty of opportunities for workers looking to be hired, especially in construction. Bricklayers, carpenters, and helpers are needed to sustain the area's residential housing growth. Thanks to the fairly steady employment, the workers can send a few hundred dollars back home to their countries of origin twice a month. But the preponderance of high-end real estate in the area is a double-edged sword. For the workers, affordable rent for local housing is an impossible dream.

The luckiest among them share small apartments. Six or eight workers share a single apartment, each paying around two hundred dollars per month in rent. Those who cannot afford even that go out to live in the ravine, under the trees, out of view of "*la migra.*"

"But pretty soon we're going to get out of here and go rent a room somewhere," a worker named Jacinto told me, optimistically. Jacinto was in his thirties and came from the state of Guerrero, in Mexico. He lived with two other laborers in a shack made of tree branches and scavenged rubber scraps used for roofing. They had piled branches and leaves over the roof of their humble abode, to camouflage it.

Inside, they slept on two mattresses that had been given to them, mounted on platforms. Outside, among the trees, they had put up clotheslines to dry their clothes after washing them in a little stream that did not look particularly clean but was all they had nearby. Toothpaste, a comb, scissors, and a hairbrush indicated the area was used for grooming. They had scavenged a table and plastic chairs, and there they ate the dinner they bought after work. Hidden from the world, they could relax, have a few beers, talk, remember. . . .

"I worked as a bricklayer back in Mexico, I earned 1,200 pesos [around $60] a week," Jacinto recalls. He also tells me he has been living in the ravine for eight months. "Here, sometimes I make eighty dollars a day, sometimes sixty. There aren't jobs every day, it's about four days a week, more or less."

Even without working every day, Jacinto earns around four times more than what he earned in Mexico. He sends all of it, minus the bare minimum needed for personal expenses, back to his wife and four children to support them.

"Yes, I'd love to see my kids, of course," he says, his gaze lost somewhere on the horizon, where the luxury homes he helps to build sit along the highway. Then he falls silent.

Jacinto's friend Gregorio also sleeps in the woods, hoping to save enough money in the next two weeks to send five hundred dollars to his wife and two children. "They pay us well here, we're getting by," Gregorio says. He has light-brown eyes, long lashes, and the ruddy, sunbaked complexion that seems to be common among many of the day laborers. "You do all the jobs, woodworking to bricklaying and cement. Sometimes people tell us *la migra* or the police are going to kick us out, but we all just stay down here when there's no work. We'll be here just a little while, maybe a year; then we'll leave and go back to Mexico."

There is nothing new about migrant workers living in ravines in northern San Diego County. Back in the 1970s and 1980s, indigenous migrants who came to work in the fields would sleep in the canyons, in primitive homes they constructed themselves from scavenged materials. At that time, most of the migration came from Oaxaca, a state in Mexico with a high population of indigenous peoples. A little while after, workers began arriving from Guerrero state. After the rise of the Zapatista National Liberation Army

(EZLN) in 1994, they started coming from Chiapas. Most of those migrants worked out in the fields for years. When the economy does very well, many of them take the chance to migrate from field work to construction.[1] During the 2008–9 financial crisis, many of these migrants had to go back to working in the fields. Many others felt they had no choice other than to return to Mexico, not under the circumstances they would have wished.

Dozens of workers gather every morning outside a liquor store in Vista, hoping to get picked up for a job doing carpentry, painting, or gardening. But the fact that many of these workers are undocumented, and that many are from indigenous communities in Mexico and Central America, makes them easy targets for exploitation and abuse. Almost everyone has had the experience of getting hired, doing the job, and then not getting paid. This can happen for a single day's work, or they may be hired for a job that takes weeks and then the boss disappears.

That's what happened to Felipe Cruz, originally from Querétaro in north-central Mexico. Felipe had a job cutting firewood and delivering it. A man had hired him to do this job several times. The man paid him part of his earnings after the job was done and promised to give him the rest in a few days. When I spoke with Felipe, he had been waiting for two months to get the remaining $650 he was owed.

"He just tells me he's going to pay me in a few days," Felipe told me outside the liquor store, sipping from a bottle of water. "I'm poor, but if he's going to treat me like that, he should get arrested. If he doesn't have the money, lock him up," he says angrily.

Juan Sajche, a human rights activist who for years has worked advising workers who have been abused and cheated by employers, visited the laborers gathered outside the liquor store that day. He explained to the group that no matter a worker's immigration status, they have the right to make a legal claim against their employer and demand payment. Juan told them he was currently helping another worker who was owed $1,200. As Juan asked for Felipe's contact information, Felipe's expression brightened a bit at the thought that somehow, he just might get justice.

In early 2014, Pablo Alvarado was flying from Los Angeles to New York. The in-flight entertainment was the movie *A Better Life*, starring Demián Bichir as a day laborer. Pablo watched the movie, and he liked it. He thought it accurately reflected what undocumented workers go through.

"Historically, the day laborer has been characterized as dirty, somebody who urinates on the sidewalk or throws trash into the street," he tells me a few days later at a screening of the movie in Panorama City, in northern Los Angeles. Tall, with a large build, light-brown skin, and a friendly smile, Pablo has an imposing physical presence that contrasts with his serene, calmly observant attitude. "It's easy for our adversaries to use that image as a symbol, but this film helps to eliminate that harmful symbology and present a human picture of us."

Pablo believes this kind of story puts a face on the tens of thousands of workers who live in anonymity. In some way, bringing their story to the big screen gives them dignity.

But a movie is not enough to change the situation for undocumented day laborers. Data from a national survey of day laborers, conducted by the University of California, Los Angeles, confirms what everyone knows but is easy to ignore: undocumented day laborers are hired to perform dangerous jobs without adequate safety measures.[2] Anyone who has seen the movie cannot help but remember Bichir climbing a palm tree. They are robbed of their wages and are often insulted, with passersby spewing hateful anti-immigrant insults and people driving by in their cars throwing things at them. For more than 85 percent of these workers, who are mostly men, the income they earn through this unregulated work is the only income they have. In a "good" month, they can earn up to $1,200, but in a bad month, it could be $500 or less. The average annual income for day laborers is $15,000, putting them at or below the poverty line in the United States.

"In concrete terms, this movie is not going to make life better for day workers who get hired off the street," says Pablo. Through the NDLON network, he organized almost a hundred screenings of the film all across the country in the weeks following its release. "But it does present another side of the story and it's a start, because with the anti-immigrant hate speech we're seeing in Alabama, or Arizona, the movie shows the human side of this horror, like the civil rights movement did for African Americans. People see themselves reflected in it, but that took many years of struggle and suffering. We're really babies at this, and the movement to reform immigration laws is going to be harder. Hollywood is understanding the workers, but Washington, DC, isn't."

On the day of the screening at Panorama High School, the crowd was in a festive mood. Teachers, students, and parents were excited to "go to the movies" in the school's auditorium. Because *A Better Life* was not widely publicized when it was first released, dozens of people came to the screening very interested in seeing it. The story genuinely moved the audience of this neighborhood where almost 70 percent of the residents are Latino. Everyone applauded at the end of the movie, some wiping tears from their eyes. Then Chris Weitz, the movie's director, came into the auditorium to participate in a forum, along with some of the actors, an undocumented student, and a few politicians campaigning for local office.

Weitz had just been in Washington, DC, where he'd held a screening for members of the US Department of Labor. It was his way of counteracting the negative stereotypes promoted by Republicans. "This is a window so people can see a way of life they know nothing about," he explained.

Of course, that was not the case for this evening's audience. José Julián, the young actor who played Luis Galindo, the son of the main character; Myisha Arellano, a student at Panorama High School who openly declared she was undocumented; the local city councilman Tony Cárdenas, who represented Panorama City: they all had experience with the undocumented life in their own families. For those in the auditorium, *A Better Life* was not a work of fiction.

"I grew up in the same neighborhood where they filmed the movie, so for me that was normal," José Julián said. His mother came to the United States undocumented from Mexico, and he grew up living a life similar to that of the character he played: the son of immigrant workers balancing the challenge of adapting to a new culture while holding fast to the values of their nuclear family. The biggest surprise to the young actor after the film's release had been finding out how many people in Los Angeles did not know what life was like for immigrant day workers.

When the panel opened the floor up to the audience for questions and comments, all heads turned toward a voice from the middle of the room. It belonged to an older man, wearing work clothes, alongside two smiling young girls.

"In the movie I identified with when the man was driving and the police came, and he was terrified," he said. His name was Guillermo, and he was originally from Mexico, had five children, and worked in construction. Part of his job was driving a truck, but, like Carlos Galindo in the movie, he was undocumented. Guillermo had been pulled over by police twice, and since he did not have a driver's license, they impounded the truck. Later, the company he worked for had to get the truck back, and he was given a court order to pay a fine. The first time the fine was five hundred dollars. The second time, it was over a thousand. "I'm sure that the first time they didn't pull me over for a violation but just because I looked Mexican," he said.

Parents and children shared stories, emotions running high. Councilman Cárdenas talked about how meaningful the movie was to him, because his father, an immigrant, had also been a gardener.

"He was one who worked hard so the next generation, people like you, could have a better life, without losing their values along the way," he said, addressing the students in the crowd. "Everyone here, if your parents came to the United States looking for a better life for their children, stand up."

Half the people in the auditorium rose from their seats, including Councilman Cárdenas.

When Omar talks about his work at NDLON, he can't hide the pride he feels. He has been working for the network for nine years. Added to his eight years at IDEPSCA, that makes thirteen years working with day laborers. He says he is grateful for the training he received as an organizer, for the great friends he made, for his love of the work, and for the satisfaction he gained promoting women's participation at the worker centers from his work at IDEPSCA. But after coordinating the program for a while, he knew he would need to find another opportunity to keep on growing.

He had already gotten to be friends with Pablo, since IDEPSCA is a part of the NDLON network, so it wasn't long before the veteran organizer asked Omar to join his organization. And from there, they have combined their activist work with the meaningful music of Los Jornaleros del Norte.

If Los Jornaleros were popular almost from the start for their talent for reflecting how people were feeling at key political moments, Donald Trump's campaign for the presidency gave them an even bigger a platform to perform their most provocative songs, portraying the feelings of an entire community. As soon as Trump announced his campaign, at the same time accusing Mexicans of being rapists and drug traffickers, Omar started to write, and Los Jornaleros started to sing.

Ay Donald Trump, Ay Donald Trump,
Arréglate el peluquín y deja de andar de hocicón
Dices, ahora resulta, que somos criminales
Narcos, violadores y no sé qué tanto más
Que es nuestra culpa que la pinche economía ande tan mal
Dices que si tú ganas nos vas a deportar
Aparte de copetudo, muy pendejo estás
Pues si nos sacan, se mueren de hambre tú y muchos más.

Hey Donald Trump, hey Donald Trump,
Fix your toupee and calm down,

Now you say we're criminals
Narcos, rapists, and I don't know what else
That it's our fault the economy's a mess
You say if you're elected you're going to deport us
Aside from a strutting rooster, you're an asshole
'Cause if you throw us out, you and lots more will starve to death.

Along with many political analysts and activists, Los Jornaleros never expected Trump to actually win the Republican Party nomination, let alone the presidential election. "I was wrong," Omar says simply. He explains the song was very harsh because he wrote it in response to Trump's statements about Mexicans. But at first it was written practically as a joke, because they never thought the American electorate would be so poorly informed and ignorant as to elect such a candidate.

"When he won, we felt horrible; a lot of things started happening," Omar says. "It had a big impact on workers like us, because people's attitudes started to change. People who thought like that man started coming out of the closet they had been hiding in. Out on street corners and at work sites, there were even more anti-immigrant attacks, like a lot of Trumps started coming out of the woodwork. The fight to get immigrants' rights recognized had taken years, and then from one day to the next, we had to fight twice as hard."

The fight has gotten results. Ever since the election results were announced, on November 8, 2016, NDLON began a series of actions that has not stopped. They held meetings attended by other organizations and concerned individuals to discuss their worries, fears, and ideas for building a defense plan for the immigrant community. The day worker network created a campaign, "Alto Trump!"[3] (Stop Trump!)—modeled on their "Alto Arizona!" campaign of 2010—encouraging members of affected communities to participate in the process of defending their civil rights in the months to come.

Activists launched a series of training sessions called "*Conoce tus derechos*" (Know your rights) to teach participants what they should do if they are attacked by hate groups or stopped by the police and asked about their immigration status; what to do in case of an immigration raid at home or at work; and how to form neighborhood watch groups to defend their communities. They also started one of the NDLON's most emotional initiatives so far: bringing Los Jornaleros del Norte to detention centers to "serenade" immigrants held in detention for being undocumented. Some of those events have been held in front of the detention center in downtown Los Angeles. They block off a small side street, and while Los Jornaleros play under the building's large windows overlooking Route 101, their supporters draw on the sidewalk with chalk, writing messages of hope and encouragement in big letters to whoever manages to see them from inside. They have done the same outside immigration court in San Diego, to support those who are having their cases heard before a judge.

"We have made our position very clear," Omar says. "While the politicians play their games and try to make a deal, one thing that could be very easy for them to do—which is in their power—would be to stop deporting people who are not a threat to the country. We have been clear on this not only with the Trump administration, but ever since the Obama administration. We have been criticized for criticizing Obama, who was the 'deporter in chief,' deporting fathers, mothers, kids. We have always asked that there be some relief while they work out an agreement: no more deportations, no more police collaboration with immigration, no raids in homes and workplaces. It's something they could do, if their priority wasn't a political benefit for their parties."

With respect to Trump in particular, Omar thinks his predominant characteristic is ignorance. He describes him as a simple man, incapable of analyzing, unable to comprehend the impact his words have on the country and on the daily lives of its communities.

"I think we are experiencing one of the saddest moments in this country's history," he says gravely. "That's why we don't stop. Our latest record is called *Chanting Down the Walls*, and we've gotten many invitations from universities, protest concerts with other artists, and we keep on serenading undocumented people. We're going to keep on supporting workers at protests. We're going to keep on supporting families so they won't be separated. We're going to keep on tearing down walls with our song."

Asómate a la ventana, te traje una serenata
Aunque estés encarcelado, mira, te canta quien te ama
Por ti me juego la vida, por liberarte me muero en la raya

¡Ay, qué leyes tan injustas! ¿Qué buscan en separarnos?
Nos juzgan de criminales por ser indocumentados
No saben que nuestras manos a ellos los tienen tragando.

Come to the window, I'm going to serenade you
Even though you're in jail, look, the one who loves you sings for you
I would risk my life for you, I would die to set you free

What unjust laws! What do they get out of separating us?
They say we're criminals for being undocumented
They don't realize they eat from our hands.

CHAPTER TWO

WHY DON'T THEY WANT US?

Claudia Amaro, forty

Tijuana, Baja California/Wichita, Kansas

Yamil Yáujar, forty-seven

Durango, Durango/Wichita, Kansas

HOW MANY TIMES can you start your life all over again from zero? If there's anyone who knows the answer to that question, it's Claudia Amaro. She had to do it for the first time when her father was murdered, when she was ten years old. She started over again for a second time when she was thirteen and her mother decided to move the whole family, including Claudia and her three sisters, to the United States, fleeing violence. She had to hit the reset button again when she was thirty and a deportation order for her husband destroyed her family and the life she had built over the past two decades, sending him, Claudia, and their US-citizen son back to Mexico, a place she no longer felt was home.

And with nothing left to lose, in the hope of getting back a little of the life that had been hers, in 2013, at thirty-seven, Claudia started over for the fourth time. She was prepared to spend as much time as necessary in a detention center in the US. She crossed the border north and at the entry gate said she wished to apply for political asylum. A few months later, her husband, Yamil, did the same. Claudia spent three weeks in detention. Yamil was locked up for two years and three months.

Back in Kansas, a place they both consider their home, Claudia and Yamil live under the ever-present shadow of possible deportation. Neither of them knows if they would be able to start over from nothing for a fifth time.

Claudia Amaro was born in Tijuana, Mexico. When she was ten years old, the family traveled to Durango state, where her father was killed under circumstances that have never been explained by law enforcement. For the next two years, the family fluctuated between anger at the authorities for not pursuing justice, and terror from the threats they started getting from the killers. Three years after her father's murder, Claudia's mother, Elvia, decided to go to Colorado with her four daughters. Claudia is the oldest sister.

She recalls, "There were very few Hispanics at the time; there were only three or four Mexicans born in Mexico at school, and the first year was really hard. I didn't know the language; I got bullied. I went without any lunch for a long time, because I didn't know the system; I didn't know how to take a tray and serve myself."

I talked to Claudia for the first time in 2013, after she reached out to me on Facebook, expressing interest in a series of reporting pieces I had written. At that time she was still living in Mexico. In a message, she told me her story in brief and said she planned to return to the US. I decided to talk to her over the phone to find out more. We have stayed in touch since then. Through our interviews I have documented her experiences from before 2013 and the path her family has taken in the years following her application for political asylum in the US.

It takes a great deal of strength for a thirteen-year-old girl to overcome the challenges that come with starting over at a new school, in a new community, in a new country, in a different language, in a completely unfamiliar structure. Claudia had that strength. With the support of some of her classmates and one of her teachers, she became the first Hispanic student to graduate from her school in Colorado with course credits in algebra. When she was seventeen, the family moved again, this time to Wichita, Kansas. There she began developing into her adult self, during what she calls "the best years of my life."

"I felt at home for the first time. I didn't miss Mexico. My sisters and I joined a youth group at church, and that's where I met my husband. We got married in 1998, when I was twenty-three. In 2000, my son was born."

Claudia's husband, Yamil, was born in Durango, Mexico. He worked as a housepainter and played soccer in a semiprofessional league. Claudia taught classes and took care of their son, Yamil Jr. Her life unfolded peacefully, until she got a call in April 2005. Her husband had been pulled over in a traffic stop, and the police discovered he was using false identification. Claudia had to go down to the police station. When she got to the station, she explained she was Yamil's wife and asked what she had to do. In response, the police took her into a room to interrogate her. They handcuffed her and brought her to immigration authorities. Claudia and Yamil were released on bond and were both facing deportation when Yamil received an order of deportation in January 2006.

"When we explained we had a six-year-old son who was a US citizen, the judge said he was still young so he could adapt to life in Mexico," Claudia told me in our first conversation over the phone, her voice breaking. Over the course of the nine months of the legal process, she and Yamil were not allowed to work. "We lost the house we had been paying for, the car, everything. We went back to Mexico with nothing."

The very hard process of adaptation she had had to face when she moved to the US was repeated once again, but this time it was twofold: Claudia and Yamil had to adjust to a country that no longer felt like home, while their son entered a completely unknown world. They went to live in Torreón, where Yamil had family. When Yamil Jr. started school, he was held back a grade because he did not speak Spanish very well. They enrolled him in a private school where he would get more individual attention, but even that did not spare him from bullying by his peers for being American. Some months before leaving Mexico, Claudia and her husband had to make a formal complaint after their son was beaten up by six other boys.

"They called him '*pocho*'; they made fun of him," Claudia says. "In first grade, he got really depressed; we had to take him to see a therapist. The therapist told me and my husband that part of the problem was we had not fully accepted that we lived in Mexico now, but how could we accept it? We had lived in Torreón for seven years, and we couldn't adapt. I don't feel American or Mexican. I feel like a human being whose home is in Wichita; that's where my family and my history is."

I could hear the anger and frustration in Claudia's voice as she talked. She told me that a few months earlier, they had been robbed at gunpoint. After seeing a gun put to his father's head, their son, thirteen at the time, began avoiding going out.

That's when Claudia and Yamil decided to find some way to go back.

"The first time I left Mexico [was] because my dad was murdered and the authorities didn't do anything. I don't want a life like that for my son. I want to go back to our home. I want my son to live the life he has a right to as a US citizen, because he's been through things here he should never have had to go through. I'm going to the US, land of immigrants, that I feel a part of. I love the Mexican people; I love how hardworking they are, but my heart has stars and stripes. I'm going home."

A few days after we talked, on July 22, 2013, Claudia and eight other young adults walked up to the border entry gate in Nogales, smiling brightly, accompanied by supporters shouting "Undocumented and unafraid!" Claudia had Yamil Jr. with her. Claudia's mother was on the other side of the gate, waiting for her grandson. He reentered his country without incident. Claudia took one last look at her son before being handcuffed, put in a van, and taken to the Eloy Detention Center in Arizona.

Eloy is in the middle of nowhere. The 115 miles stretching between Phoenix and Tucson, Arizona's two biggest cities, are pure desert and sky. The detention center is right at the halfway point. To get to Eloy, you have to drive on Interstate 10, the seemingly endless highway that spans the country from the Pacific Coast in California to the Atlantic in Florida. Sometimes the wind whips up and pelts the cars on the road with sheets of desert sand. Or the sun, beating down for twelve hours a day, heats up the pavement to such an extreme it causes car tires to burst. At the sign for Casa Grande, it's time to take a left turn onto a dusty road and drive for another fifteen miles until you reach a complex of squat cement buildings planted crudely in the heart of the desert, consisting of three prisons and the immigrant detention center. These four buildings hold five thousand lives in a state of suspended animation, contained by barbed wire and electric fences.

Eloy is one of six detention centers in Arizona operated by CoreCivic, the company that manages most of the private prisons in the United States. Previously called the Corrections Corporation of America, the company changed its name to CoreCivic just a few days before Donald Trump won the presidential election in 2016. The detention center has 1,596 beds and is filled with men and women accused of being on this side of the border without a piece of paper. For thirty years, CoreCivic has earned millions of dollars in profits for holding people who have been detained while they wait for their cases to be decided by a judge.

In the six months after November 8, 2016, the day Trump won the election, the stock prices of CoreCivic and GEO, the other major private prison company running immigrant detention centers, saw gains of over 100 percent.[1] Beyond the financial windfall this brought the two companies, it meant their futures were secure, with plenty of business on the horizon.

Four months earlier, during the Obama administration, Deputy Attorney General Sally Yates issued a directive to the Federal Bureau of Prisons to reduce their government contracts with private prisons, with the goal of ultimately phasing them out entirely. After that announcement, stock prices for CoreCivic and GEO plummeted by 40 percent. Two months later, just as the presidential campaign reached its apex, CoreCivic announced that it would have to make staff cuts in order to balance their budget. Trump and his opponent, Hillary Clinton, had staked out opposing positions.

Clinton vowed to uphold the decision to cut private prison contracts, while Trump maintained that the private prison and detention system was good for the country.

Yates's decision to cut the contracts was based on a Department of Justice report summarizing the dramatic growth of the immigrant detention system in the United States—an 800 percent increase between 1980 and 2013—and showing a decrease in the number of immigrants in detention from 220,000 in 2013 to 195,000 in 2016.[2] According to the report, the high costs associated with paying private prison companies were no longer necessary. The private prisons also had a history of accusations of abuse, human rights violations, labor exploitation, and a lack of transparency, some of which resulted in fines levied against the companies and the closings of some installations.

In spite of this, on February 23, 2017, the new attorney general, Jeff Sessions, reversed Yates's order, injecting new life into CoreCivic and GEO. Sessions argued that maintaining contracts with private prisons and detention centers conformed with the "future needs" of the federal corrections system. It was most likely no coincidence that both GEO and CoreCivic supported the Republican Party and Trump with donations during the presidential campaign: GEO donated a total of $673,000, while CoreCivic donated at least $130,000.[3]

In the years to come, at least during Trump's first term in office, 15,000 new immigration agents are expected to be hired to detain immigrants, even though as of 2017 there were only 301 judges in the entire country hearing immigration cases to handle over 500,000 cases pending, not to mention all of the cases resulting from future detentions. This means more immigrants will be held in detention and, therefore, there will be a greater need for private detention centers; longer periods spent in detention for those seeking a chance to stay in the country or simply to save their lives; and higher profits than ever for the private prison companies.

When Yamil Yáujar arrived in Eloy, he knew what was in store. His wife, Claudia, had been held in the same place seven weeks earlier. I heard the story from two points of view, first from Claudia, talking by phone from Kansas, where she returned after a judge released her on her own recognizance while her asylum case was pending. Then I spoke in person with Yamil in Eloy's visiting room, where I was allowed a visit with him in February 2015. Claudia and Yamil shared details of their shared life with me, memories they'd held fast to over the course of the two years and three months they were separated.

In the visiting room at the detention center, where around two dozen families gather to spend an hour with a loved one detained for crossing the border undocumented, or for working without proper documentation, or, as in Yamil's case, for turning oneself in to immigration authorities to apply for asylum, Yamil tells me his side of the story. We are sitting in the back of the room shaped like a shoe box, facing each other across a table. In this room, adults are not allowed to sit next to each other. Yamil, forty-four at the time of our visit, tells me that in the years his family lived in Torreón, he and Claudia had a hard time getting jobs, and the violence unleashed during President Felipe Calderón's six-year term had begun to ravage the region. Shoot-outs and murders became a normal part of their daily life. Then, cases of extortion proliferated. Until one day it was their turn.

After years of hard work, Yamil had opened up his own small business, a hamburger stand. He had only been open for a few weeks, and he had a secondhand pickup truck he used for the business. On January 26, 2012, which happened to be Yamil Jr.'s birthday, two men came by his hamburger stand and asked him who owned the truck. Yamil told them it was his. The men told him they had to take it, because it had been reported stolen. Claudia offered to show them their title to the truck, to no avail. The men forced Yamil into the truck and drove off with him. A few hours later, Yamil's family got a call demanding a ransom of a thousand dollars in exchange for his release. His family got the ransom together, and Yamil came home. A few weeks after his kidnapping, the men came back and stole the truck at gunpoint.

"After that, for three days, they kept passing by my stand. I had to close it," Yamil recalls, sadness in his eyes. But he is not bitter or defeated. The khaki jumpsuit uniform he wears makes him look even thinner. His short hair, shaved close to his scalp, accentuates his lively eyes, like two black cherries.

A few months later, Yamil and Claudia had to go to the public ministry of Torreón to file a complaint because their son had been beaten up by several other boys who called him "gringo" and "*pocho*," derogatory terms. While they made their statement, Yamil recognized one of the police officers there. He was one of the men who had stolen his truck. After that, it wasn't hard to make the decision they had to make.

In July 2013, Claudia and Yamil Jr. went to the border gate and she declared her intention to apply for political asylum. A few weeks later, Yamil did the same. In the US, the political asylum application process takes five years on average to complete. While the asylum case is pending, it is at a judge's discretion whether to release the applicant on their own recognizance. Claudia was released after three weeks spent in detention, but Yamil was not. And even though he could have signed for his voluntary release at any time to return to Mexico, he decided to stay in detention.

After a long pause, his shining eyes trained on mine, Yamil tells me why a man would choose to spend over two years locked up in a detention center rather than go back to his country: "It's worth it for my son. He misses me right now, but he can live in peace. In Mexico, we couldn't live."

In mid-June 2017, Yamil and Claudia were counting down to an important day: August 29. That is when Yamil had a date in immigration court in Kansas City in what could be the first in a long series of appearances before a judge to move his asylum case forward. When asylum applicants appear before a judge, they have to demonstrate a credible fear of physical harm or death if they are returned to their country.

If the judge determines there is a credible fear, then the case proceeds, one step closer to the granting of asylum. But if the judge does not find sufficient evidence, then the applicant, in this case Yamil, could be taken into custody right there—as he was in 2005—and deported to Mexico immediately. For Claudia and Yamil, the old fears resurface, because this time could turn out the same as before. In that sense, Claudia and Yamil are different from other undocumented immigrants, because they have already experienced the worst-case scenario, and it scarred their family forever.

Ever since they were released from detention—Claudia in June 2013 and Yamil in December 2015—they have lived in Kansas with their son. Claudia's first court date was initially scheduled for late 2019, but because of changes made in immigration courts under the new administration, another judge was assigned to her case and the date was moved up to January 2018. Then she was rescheduled to 2020. In any case, they have the same fear: this family's anxiety is directly related to the changes the Trump administration has started to make in the criteria for prioritizing immigrants vulnerable to deportation.

In 2011, under instructions from President Obama, a document was published by immigration authorities known as the "Morton Memo," referring to John Morton, director of Immigration and Customs Enforcement (ICE). The memo said that, since the agency only had the capacity to deport four hundred thousand people annually, immigration agents should focus their efforts on those individuals who posed a danger to the country. Priority should be given to people representing a threat to national security, meaning those with criminal records or ties to terrorism and, in some cases, those with prior minor offenses, at the discretion of immigration authorities.

Since the beginning of the Trump administration, policy changes in how immigration laws are applied indicate that authorities may use their discretion to qualify any violation of the law as a "crime," widely and arbitrarily broadening the spectrum of people who could be considered a "danger" to the country. People like Yamil, who was charged with using false documents and has a previous deportation on his record, could be deemed a threat to national security.

Although Claudia's concerns are certainly legitimate, this broad application of discretion by immigration authorities is not completely new. During the Obama administration, judicial discretion led to the deportation of people who did not meet the standards of the Morton Memo. As is well known, during the course of Obama's eight years in office, more than three million people were deported, significantly more than the two million deportations under George W. Bush and the 870,000 under Bill Clinton, his immediate predecessors in the Oval Office.[4]

During the first year of his administration, pro-immigrant organizations warned that by his second term, Obama, the president who had centered his election campaign on themes of "hope" and "change," could become the "deporter in chief," a play on the president's role as commander in chief. During his first three years in office, the number of deportations reached 390,000; from year four to six, that figure surpassed 400,000. In Obama's last two years in office, although the number of deportations declined somewhat, there were still no fewer than 300,000. On average, 1,100 people were deported every single day during Obama's two terms.

Aside from the sheer magnitude of the number, the deportation issue became a thorn in Obama's side because of the profiles of the people being deported. A study by the Transactional Records Analysis Clearinghouse (TRAC) at Syracuse University published in 2014 found that of all the people deported by ICE in 2013, 41 percent had not committed any type of crime and only 12 percent had been charged with a Level 1 felony or greater. Of this last group, 25 percent had only committed the crime of unlawfully reentering the country. An analysis of the nationalities of those deported in the same report found that over 65 percent were Mexican.[5]

Many of the deportations carried out under Obama's administration involved people such as Claudia and Yamil, parents of US-citizen children. Between July 2010 and October 2012, immigration authorities deported two hundred thousand parents with US-citizen children.[6] This is double the number of such deportations carried out from 1997 to 2007, according to a 2012 ICE report.[7]

During one of our phone conversations, Claudia told me she shuddered at the thought of Yamil's upcoming court date in August. "The whole thing makes me think about what happened before. That time, when we were in court, Yamil was released on

$10,000 bond. But when his first court date came up, they said there wasn't sufficient evidence and he was taken into custody right there. All I have is my faith in God and my community, because we've worked so hard and I believe we have their support. We know the senators, the representatives, the mayor, the police chief, the people."

Comparing their two cases, Claudia has a better chance of gaining legal status than Yamil. She has not been deported before, and she returned to Mexico voluntarily to be with her husband. And according to the criteria of some immigration judges, the longer someone has lived in the US, the better the chances of being allowed to stay. If, at her court date in 2018, the judge would have decided to deny her asylum application and deport her, or if that happens at her next date, in 2020, Claudia has some recourse. In January 2021, Jamil Jr. will turn twenty-one, at which point he could petition for residency for his parents.

Claudia tells me that after Yamil Jr.'s experiences living in Mexico and everything he has been through—returning to the US when he was thirteen and living with his grandmother for a few weeks while his mother was held in detention, and then waiting two years for his father to finally be released—her son does not like to discuss the subject. She draws some comfort from the fact that if she and her husband are obligated to return to Mexico, at least Yamil Jr. will be old enough to decide where he wants to live. That is a tremendous relief. In the years they lived in Mexico, Claudia often felt guilty for having taken her son to live in a hostile environment, even though as a US citizen he had the right to remain in his country.

The family has rebuilt their life in Wichita. Claudia works as a family liaison at a school, helping parents get more involved, and started a translation and interpreting business with her sisters. Yamil started his own housepainting company in mid-2016. And not only is he not "stealing jobs," as anti-immigrant rhetoric about Mexicans would have us believe, he is generating jobs: he has hired three people to work for him. Yamil Jr., now seventeen, is doing well in school and would like to become an engineer one day.

"I will support him in whatever he decides to do," Claudia tells me. "Right now he loves school, he has his friends, he plays soccer, and he's very excited about going to college. He has a girlfriend he adores, and he doesn't want to leave Wichita. My son suffered so much there [in Mexico]. He was at five different schools; it was really bad. I feel good about giving him the happiness now that he didn't have in those years."

Complementing her work in school, and as an outgrowth of everything she has learned in recent years, is Claudia's work as an organizer for the undocumented community in Wichita, including sharing her personal experience with people who feel threatened by stricter immigration enforcement under the Trump administration. She also tries to talk with far-right conservatives who hold strong beliefs with little or no knowledge of immigrant rights. She offers an example: in Kansas, many people are very pro-life and strongly oppose abortion rights. Claudia tries to explain to them that if they are truly pro-life, they should know that every person is born with the right to migrate. Claudia says that many Latinos vote along the same party lines as Republicans in the state because of religious or personal beliefs, even though conservative politics sometimes give no consideration to defending ethnic minorities.

"I tell them the same people who are against immigration are against education, decent jobs, helping the poorest Americans; they want to own the entire country. I challenge them to find out how their representatives vote on education, immigration, and what their relationships are to the big corporations who lobby and make big campaign contributions, and in exchange [how] legislators act in the interest of those companies. In Kansas, a bill was presented to reduce corporate taxes, while initiatives that would have helped the poor get access to education were defeated. They don't want us educated, because they need us to just be cheap labor."

Claudia acknowledges that even in Kansas, where organizing is harder and there is more resistance than in other states, activism undertaken by pro-immigrant organizations in recent years has had some positive results. People are better informed. She tells me

that some media outlets have stopped using language that crimi-
nalizes immigrants, no longer using the word "illegal" to describe
an undocumented person. Although there is still intolerance, many
Americans are supportive. Claudia mentions a man who closed his
business one day because his workers had not shown up. He went
to their homes, concerned. They explained that they were taking
part in a one-day action to demonstrate the effects on the workforce of the absence of immigrants. Hearing this, their employer
gave them his wholehearted support and posed for a photo next to
a poster with the slogan "A Day Without Immigrants."

"I love this country because of people like that," Claudia says
emphatically.

When Claudia thinks about the future, she pictures herself still
working at the school and being involved as an activist. She currently hosts a radio show, *Planeta Venus*, where she discusses general interest topics from a woman's perspective. She also works with
Movimiento Cosecha, a group that promotes immigrant rights, and
runs a *Conoce tus derechos* (Know your rights) workshop in which
she draws on her personal experience helping families come up with
a plan in the event that they are stopped by police: they must have a
plan in place for their legal defense, to alert their support networks
and even local and national media if necessary.

Claudia assures me that to her, the Trump administration is
no different from previous administrations when it comes to
deportations.

"The separation of families is the same, the pain is the same,"
she says. "I would like to think that now people see the enemy
more clearly and will try to prepare themselves more, psychologically, for how to respond about their immigration status. But as
far as the act of deportation itself, I don't see any difference, because it's the same suffering for somebody deported ten years ago
or somebody deported yesterday, or a month from now. Trump
talks about legality, but sometimes what is legal is not necessarily
what is right. . . . [S]lavery was [once] legal, but that doesn't mean
it was right. I would like to say to him, 'I hope you never have to

leave your country. If you did, you would know what it's like to live under a microscope, listening to other people's opinions when they have no idea of what you've had to go through.'"

Claudia is trying to overcome what she's been through, but she does not forget. To avoid separating her family, she says she lost valuable years, time she could have devoted to her personal development.

"I learned a lot, but I felt lost in my personal life. In Mexico I felt like I was trapped in a bottle. Here, I feel free. I know this country isn't perfect, but this is where I belong, this is my home. I am proud to be Mexican, but here at home I have the freedom to do what I do, and I know I would not have that in Mexico. I couldn't do what I'm doing here: talking to people and organizing them, saying whatever I want."

Before we wrapped up our conversation, Claudia told me that once while she was talking to an American woman, she asked her, "Why doesn't the US want us?" The woman replied, "Fortunately, the government's policies don't reflect the whole country."

CHAPTER THREE

OAXACALIFORNIA

Odilia Romero, forty-six
San Bartolomé Zoogocho, Oaxaca/Los Angeles, California

"GOOD AFTERNOON, SENATOR SANDERS. My name is Odilia Romero, indigenous Bene Xhon."

Standing onstage at the Casa del Mexicano in Boyle Heights, a neighborhood in East Los Angeles, Odilia holds a microphone in one hand and in the other her speech for Bernie Sanders, then a candidate for the Democratic Party's nomination for president. It was May 4, 2016, and in the auditorium beneath the fifty-foot-high domed ceiling, four hundred people had gathered, a mix of pro-immigrant organizations, young activists, and members of the Latina community.

"I come from a sacred place where now very few people live; it's a ghost town, because most of us now are here in Los Angeles," Odilia says. She is dressed in a white skirt and blouse embroidered with brightly colored flowers, very typical of Zoogocho, the community she comes from. She explains that while indigenous communities are rich in culture and natural resources, every day indigenous peoples are forced to migrate north as a consequence of US agricultural policies.

"When we stand up for our land and human rights, we're threatened with death by the Mexican police and army," she says. We go from being landowners to becoming low-wage workers. But in the United States, we are in the same condition: we are over 20 percent of the agricultural labor force in California, but we face discrimination, structural racism, and labor exploitation, along with racism from our other Mexican brothers and sisters."

Sitting on a stool on the stage with one foot on the floor, wearing a light blue shirt with rolled-up sleeves, slightly hunched over, his hair a tousled mess as usual, Senator Sanders looks at Odilia and listens respectfully, sometimes looking surprised by what he hears.

"What will you and your team do to build a broad, inclusive coalition that acknowledges our diverse community and create policies that recognize indigenous peoples' right to stay home and make immigration voluntary instead of a forced necessity?" Odilia asks. "Will you prohibit any future agreements like NAFTA that increase unemployment, low wages, poverty, and displacement of indigenous people all over?

"Thank you, and welcome to Oaxacalifornia."

Odilia is a *Bene Xhon*, which means "Zapotec people." She was born in Zoogocho, in Oaxaca state's northern mountains—"where we walk in the clouds"—in 1971, at the beginning of the decade that would bring the devaluation of the dollar and the decline of rural life in Mexico. Odilia clearly remembers the first wave of migration from her community. A flatbed truck would come every week on market days, and along with the market vendors, the truck would take people who were going away in search of opportunity. "A truck full of empty baskets, and empty men and women, hoping to fill their wallets they would leave behind their people, their language, their traditions, and their hearts to go over to 'the other side of the fence' for a few years," Odilia once wrote, remembering those years.

Eventually her day to climb aboard the truck came. She arrived in Los Angeles in 1981, where her family was already waiting. She does not remember the exact date, but she does recall "the ugly buildings I saw here on Sixth and Union Streets," her first impression of the city. She was ten years old, and she was struck by the jarring change in her environment, going from living in a natural landscape, next to a river lined with trees, to spending her time inside in a room she rarely left, in a neighborhood where she was not allowed to go outside to play.

"It was the worst thing that had ever happened to me. I think I suffered from depression, but I didn't know it."

Like most children who come to the United States to live, Odilia learned English quickly. When she was only fourteen, she even acted as an interpreter for another native of Oaxaca preparing for a state exam to be licensed as a hairdresser: he did not speak English well, and knowing that Odilia could speak Zapotec and some Spanish, he asked her parents if she could help him. When he got his license, he offered to pay Odilia for her help, but her parents refused. At the time, Odilia couldn't imagine that being an interpreter could actually be a professional career, but now she remembers that experience as her first real interpreting job.

As is still the custom in many indigenous communities, Odilia married young, when she was just fifteen. Her first child, Janet, a girl, was born when Odilia was sixteen. For five years, Odilia lived the traditional life like so many women in her community, staying at home and raising a family. But she wanted more. She separated from her husband and began making a new life for herself and her daughter.

"There was a time when my people from Zoogocho looked down on me because I had left my husband and because I didn't go to the parties. So I started doing other things," Odilia says, remembering how her community tended to ostracize women who broke from traditional roles, even in the United States. "My parents did not speak Spanish very well then, and neither did I; a lot of people didn't. I knew there was a need [for interpreters], but I never thought of it as a career. We had a restaurant, and a young man who came there to eat introduced me to Gaspar Rivera-Salgado, one of the founders of the Frente."

Odilia was referring to the Frente Indígena de Organizaciones Binacionales (FIOB), which describes itself as a coalition of organizations, communities, and individuals based in Oaxaca, Baja California, and California, seeking to contribute to the development and self-determination of migrant and nonmigrant indigenous peoples, and to fight for the defense of human rights and for justice and gender equality on a binational level.[1] When she found out about the work they did, Odilia joined a nonprofit associated with FIOB, the Centro Binacional para el Desarrollo Indígena Oaxaquenno (CBDIO), where she got a job. Once there, she learned that migrants from other indigenous communities, like the Mixtecs and Triquis, had needs even greater than those of her community from Zoogocho, which had an established support and solidarity network in Los Angeles.

Mexico is a multicultural, multilingual country where seven million people speak indigenous languages. Of those, more than a million speak only one of seventy-two indigenous languages, and no Spanish.[2] This population is concentrated in a few of Mexico's thirty-one states. Oaxaca, which, along with neighboring states Guerrero and Chiapas, is one of the three poorest states in the country, is also the state with the largest indigenous population, at over 1.5 million. With over sixteen ethnolinguistic groups, four out of every ten inhabitants of the state speak an indigenous language, and 14 percent of the population do not speak Spanish. This figure is even higher among women: of every ten people who only speak an indigenous language, six are women.[3] In recent decades, members of these groups have increasingly been migrating to the United States. According to current estimates, 500,000 indigenous Oaxacans live in the United States, and 70 percent of them live in California.[4]

Aside from a lack of documents, for migrants who do not speak Spanish or English, it's a challenge just to find interpreters to help with carrying out official business—with the government, signing contracts, or when seeking medical attention or legal help, sometimes in what could be matters of life or death. States like California generally provide interpreters for non-English speakers, but Mexicans are assigned Spanish-language interpreters. Because of the work FIOB started to do on this issue and some other projects on indigenous languages—like legal orientation for immigrant families and entrepreneurship workshops for indigenous women—authorities recognized the need for interpreters fluent in indigenous languages.

"The Frente has been doing this for twenty-five years," Odilia points out. "The first interpreter training was for the community in San Juan Bautista, they did not have this kind of support. Then they did a second with the Mayans, and later the languages needed were Mixtec, Zapotec, and Quiché. We more or less met that demand, but for a long time there have been other languages that need interpreters and we are overwhelmed."

The need for interpreters is most acute in two places: hospitals and courts. Odilia has worked in both, interpreting from English to Spanish or to Zapotec, the language of many of her fellow Oaxacans who have settled in Southern California. The matter has grown more complicated as migration has diversified, in terms of places of origin as well as points of destination. In places where migration of indigenous peoples is just beginning, finding interpreting services is practically impossible.

Odilia emphasizes that the worst part is not the lack of services, but that some businesses offering interpreting services to government agencies do not have a full command of the languages they offer, or their dialects. Aside from being a kind of fraud that is very hard to prove—if no one speaks the language, how can an inaccurate translation be identified?—this poses a real danger to the community.

"If you don't know how to accurately describe a certain kind of cancer, for example; if you can't explain the instructions for a prescription; if you are not familiar with the vocabulary used in immigration court; if you're not prepared emotionally, psychologically, to deliver the news that a baby is going to die, then how do you do it?" she says. "It's a disaster."

Dozens of cases have ended in disaster. One of the most widely known is that of Cirila Balthazar Cruz, a Oaxacan woman from the Chatino community. Cirila lived in Mississippi, where she worked in a Chinese restaurant and shared a room with other migrants. She was pregnant and went into labor one night in November 2008. She spoke no English and knew just a few words of Spanish. She flagged down a police car that took her to the hospital, where she gave birth to Rubí Juana Baltazar Cruz.

While she recovered from the birth, Cirila was visited by a Puerto Rican interpreter who asked her several questions in Spanish about her socioeconomic situation. Later, Cirila would say she could not answer her because "she talked really fast and I didn't understand."[5] The interpreter determined that Cirila was not fit to be a mother, and the Department of Social Services assumed custody of her infant daughter. Cirila was released from the hospital without her baby. A few days later, a couple who was interested in adopting her was given temporary custody.

The case went to court, where the interpreter justified her finding of child neglect on Cirila's part, claiming that the patient offered sex in exchange for housing, that her husband had abandoned her, that she wanted to give her daughter up for adoption and go back to Mexico, and that she was an undocumented immigrant who had already "abandoned" two other children in Mexico. A series of torturous court appearances followed for Cirila, without an interpreter who spoke Chatino, the only language she knew. Fortunately, a civil rights organization in Mississippi contacted FIOB in California and it found a Chatino interpreter for Cirila. Then, through the interpreter, she could finally explain that she never wanted to give her daughter up for adoption and that she had never abandoned her children in Mexico but had left them in her mother's care while she went to the United States to work and provide them with a better life, like so many migrants do. The local court was unmoved and terminated Cirila's parental rights, even denying her visitation privileges. A long year had to pass while the Southern Poverty Law Center waged a winning legal battle on her behalf. Finally, Cirila got her daughter back.

There are many cases of men and women in California who have been found guilty of crimes and served prison sentences as a consequence of a communication gap between the defendants and the courts.[6] To address this, in 1996, FIOB started the Project of Indigenous Interpreters with the aim of training indigenous migrants in interpretation techniques, legal terminology, and professional ethics. In 2006, twelve indigenous women who spoke Mixtec, Zapotec, Triqui, and Chatino, in addition to Spanish and in some cases English, received interpreter training, with an emphasis on health care so they could work in clinics and hospitals. Odilia was among them.

It's Friday in Los Angeles, and the heat announcing summer's arrival can be felt rising in the air. Odilia, who I have known for several years through my work writing on migration issues in Southern California, meets me at a café a half block from Children's Hospital, where she is working as an interpreter. The hospital is full of stories of pain, and of hope. Founded as a nonprofit in 1901, it is now considered the best children's hospital in California and one of the top ten in the United States.[7] Children and their families who come to the hospital generally receive unwelcome news involving organ transplants or intensive treatments for diseases like cancer and leukemia, but they also get resources to support them. For families who do not speak English, one of those resources is an interpreter's services.

The hospital has a permanent staff of Spanish-English interpreters and hires freelancers such as Odilia when it needs additional people to translate the type of Zapotec she speaks (there are several variants of that language). Of the freelancers, Odilia is the only one who speaks an indigenous language. She is often asked to try to find other interpreters through her networks. She has seen families at the hospital from Oaxaca and Guatemala who speak dialects of Zapotec that she does not understand, as well as Chinantecan, Mixe, Mam, Kanjobal, and Chibchan. If the patient and his or her family can communicate only in one of those six languages, no interpreters are available.

As for courtrooms, recent months have seen rising numbers of indigenous peoples from Guatemala: Zapotecs from the southern sierra who, Odilia tells me, started migrating because of mining concessions in their areas that made the fields no longer arable as a result of unplanned water exploitation and soil contamination, among other factors. Another growing group is the Triqui, fleeing political conflicts in their region. For the Raramuris, from northwest Mexico, their problems stem from their location near the US border: narco-traffickers use them as drug mules, and when caught, they have been sentenced to prison, even though they could not understand anything that was said at their trials for lack of an interpreter.

"Indigenous communities are faced with the structural racism of the justice, health-care, and education systems in the United States; with the language barrier on top of that, but also cultural issues, because in our communities, justice is not punitive," Odilia explains. "The other day we were in a workshop for training new interpreters, and the instructor asked, 'How would you say "judge"?' There were Quichés, Zapotecs, and Mixtecs, and we thought it would be something like 'the big man,' or 'the principal,' or 'the elderly man,' because that's who has authority—the role of judge does not exist in our communities. 'And how would you say "court"?' That would be 'the big man's house.' 'How would you say "prison"?' Iron house, or metal house. 'And how would you say "juvenile court"?' Then that would be the house for children who do not walk straight, because you're not going to say they did something bad or good. In our cosmic vision, when the child does not walk straight ahead, there is time to put him on the right path. It's not like the punitive system in the United States that throws you in jail because you stole a pizza."

In addition to the differences in customs and word usage in indigenous communities, the justice system in the United States is also quite different from the Mexican system. The team Odilia works with is currently developing a glossary to help people express ideas in indigenous languages, because in both the medical and legal fields, complex terms that come up can be very challenging for interpreters.

"In the hospitals, there are illnesses like muscular atrophy. What is that? Sometimes you don't even know how to say it in Spanish. The cases that come to Children's Hospital are sensitive." Odilia reminds me that because of patient confidentiality, she cannot go into detail about specific patients. "And you realize there are people who don't understand, they don't even know what the diagnosis is. The worst thing that I've ever seen happen there was seeing how someone's son died, and they never had an interpreter; they never knew why he died. They never knew why a resuscitation team of twenty doctors came into the room to try to revive him. No one could explain what they were doing to their child."

For years, the issue of interpreting for non-English-speaking parents has come up not only in hospitals and courts but also in schools and government offices. Often, children who grow up speaking English at school and Spanish at home act as interpreters for their parents, helping them fill out official forms, translating instructions from operating manuals, and sometimes serving as interpreters in their own cases at schools and hospitals, which can of course be problematic.

When our conversation touches on this subject, Odilia recalls an incident from her own childhood. When she was in middle school, a boy was picking on her, and she responded by hitting him with a stapler, injuring him. The school suspended Odilia for a week and called her parents. But her parents did not speak English, and the school's principal did not speak Spanish or Zapotec, so it fell to Odilia to translate for the principal. Instead of reporting her suspension, Odilia told her parents that because of her outstanding work, the school had given her a week's vacation.

"These things still happen today. I see it at the hospital; I see it [in] the courts; I see it at school: the child is the interpreter, and of course that is not the best person to ask to be your interpreter, especially at school!" Odilia says with a laugh, remembering her own example. "Imagine what can happen with doctors. You can't say to a kid, 'Tell your mother she has cancer and she's got six months to live,' but that is what is happening on a national level, in Spanish and even more with indigenous languages, because there's no alternative."

Paradoxically, the access these children have to bilingualism and even trilingualism, in Odilia's case, as well as the level of responsibility they assume from a young age, means they have far greater academic and professional opportunities than their parents' generation. During her speech to Bernie Sanders, Odilia underscored this point.

"We have integrated into US culture. We vote. We have graduates from Berkeley, Harvard, Stanford, and UCLA, not only with bachelor's degrees but also with master's and PhDs. We contribute economically and culturally to the social fabric of the United States. We are proud to call ourselves Americans, because we are the original owners of the American continent, yet we are also proud to be a part of this great country. We also have the right to be treated equally."

An interesting characteristic of this generation of Oaxacans who have successfully taken their places in the upper echelons of US society—including Janet, the daughter Odilia had when she was just fifteen, who graduated from UC Berkeley—is that they maintain a fierce pride in their indigenous identity. This marks a clear difference from the previous generation. Many people over forty remember their childhoods growing up as Latino immigrants as a time when their culture was not viewed positively: they had to try to speak English, eat what everyone else ate, wear what everyone else wore. Many parents even forbade their children to speak Spanish so they would not be seen as "different."

"Now, kids bring their lunch to school and they can bring a torta or nopales, and it's normal," says Odilia. "In the eighties, no one would have dared, at least I wouldn't have. I wouldn't have dreamed of eating beans in front of all those kids who thought I was weird because I didn't know Spanish or English. They made fun of me. They said 'You're an Indian,' and I would just say 'Uh-huh,' because I didn't understand. I never would have imagined that we would get to the point where kids could go to school with their quesadillas or their beans."

Odilia believes cultivating pride in one's heritage helps children deal with identity issues that affect many migrant families. She has a seven-year-old son, Bianí, and an eight-year-old granddaughter, Amelie. A few weeks earlier, they told Odilia they wanted to talk to her about something, and Amelie said, "Grandma, you're gonna teach us Zapotec; we can't let it die." Bianí added, "I want to learn, too, because we're from Zoogocho." How could she say no? Odilia set to work, and now she posts videos on her Facebook page, "How do you say [animal name] in Zapotec?"—illustrated and explained by Bianí and Amelie.

Although access to an indigenous-language interpreter is often complicated by the lack of qualified people, it is also closely tied to public-policy development by the federal government, state governments, and on the municipal level, and to budgets that pass to support those policies. In most cases, one determining factor for the allocation of resources for certain programs and services—schools, hospitals, police departments—is the information gathered by the US Census.

The directors of the Frente Indígena de Organizaciones Binacionales and the Centro Binacional para el Desarrollo Indígena Oaxaqueño understand this very well. In 2010, when the most recent US Census was taken, the organizations launched a campaign urging their communities to participate and to specify their indigenous origins on the forms. With higher participation, the aim was to get a more accurate estimate of the number of indigenous peoples living in the US and, therefore, gain better representation and services for them in the public sphere. Flyers and educational materials were produced and distributed at workshops and public events, and assistance in filling out the Census form was provided in indigenous languages including Mixtec, Zapotec, and Triqui for those who could not fill it out in Spanish—the Census Bureau provides the questionnaire in that language and sixty others.

In some counties in California, including Fresno where a large part of the migrant indigenous community working in the agricultural fields is located, the Census Bureau sends in a team specializing in building community alliances to visit the fields, to establish trust and encourage people to fill in the questionnaire regardless of their immigration status. And of course, one of the most strategic community alliances was with the members of FIOB and CBDIO and their interpreter program, through the Census campaign they had launched independently.

As always, a major challenge was finding the right word, because although "census" translates to *censo* in Spanish, no such word exists in indigenous languages. They decided to use *kavi* in Mixtec and *walab* in Zapotec; both words mean "count" or "recount." In its campaign, FIOB stressed the importance of answering questions 8 and 9 on the Census questionnaire: the first, on country of origin—Mexico—and the second, on belonging to a Native American ethnic group—Mixtec, Triqui, Zapotec, Purépecha.

"For years we have been ignored by the Census, by institutions; they commit statistical genocide with indigenous communities both here and in Mexico," Odilia told me at the time.[8]

"Federal money sometimes doesn't get to us because we don't have the documentation to get the resources they talk about. Now our biggest challenge is people who can't read or write. It's going to be impossible for us to count all the indigenous people because we are completely dependent on volunteers, but we'll do the best we can. We have a huge challenge ahead of us."

Talking in the café during a break from her work, Odilia and I remember how over all these years her organization has worked to forge connections with US authorities—the Census is a good example, but there are dozens more. FIOB has built bridges and created alliances with police departments including the LAPD, which has a cultural-sensitivity program for officers working in communities with large numbers of Latinos and/or indigenous peoples. FIOB also works with authorities in small cities such as Greenfield, in California's Central Valley, where the Triqui community has been settled for over ten years.

Over the past few decades, FIOB has also tried to work with authorities in Mexico, although it has not always gotten a positive response due to a lack of will to assign human or economic resources for their communities abroad. Nonetheless, FIOB has received calls from the Mexican Consulate in Los Angeles asking if FIOB could provide interpreters for the office or in the courts.

Odilia grows indignant when we get to this last subject. It amazes her that years have gone by and Mexican congressional representatives and governors cannot make even a minimal effort to support the indigenous community, which keeps Mexican states' economies afloat with the remittances they send back. She is even more offended by these politicians' self-righteous, hollow statements following Trump's election about how it's time to protect the migrants.

"Tell me, how is it that I can sit down with Charlie Beck [chief of the Los Angeles Police Department] at a forum on indigenous communities, and Mexican politicians, senators, deputies come to say they want to open a dialogue with us, as if we were stupid or defenseless?" says Odilia. "We already have a dialogue with [Eric] Garcetti [mayor of Los Angeles], with councilmen, and we've gotten much more help from them than from these people who come promoting some help that doesn't exist, that's good for nothing. It bothers me that these politicians come here to wash themselves clean with Trump. Of course we don't support him, but don't blame him for your faults: you passed policies that caused the migration of indigenous people, so you're more to blame than he is. We have defended ourselves on our own—my people have been here for thirty years and we've never asked for anything. We have financially supported ourselves here, and we've sent remittances home to improve our communities. We have done it, not the governments."

Odilia believes that in spite of the extremist policies Trump promotes, the actual situation for indigenous migrants is not going to change much: the politics of exclusion, the discrimination, harassment, and abuse have always been there.

"For indigenous peoples, it doesn't matter who's in the government; we will still be indigenous. The Mexicans are not going to change because Trump is the president; to them, we're still '*el indígena*.' Here in the United States, even Mexicans discriminate against you because they see you wearing a huipil; the racism is very internalized. And I have said to them flat out, 'Now you're feeling bad about racist comments against Mexicans, but we hear them every day from you. You're getting a taste of your own medicine.'"

CHAPTER FOUR

A QUESTION OF HONOR

Alberto B. Mendoza, forty-six
Ensenada, Baja California/Los Angeles, California

ONE OF THE MOST infamous scandals to hit turn-of-the-century high society in Mexico City happened on November 18, 1901, during President Porfirio Diaz's reign. That night, police raided a party at a private home and arrested forty-one gay men, nineteen of them dressed in drag. Officers violently burst into the house, and to publicly humiliate the partygoers, forced them to march through the streets. They were called bums, thieves, and faggots, and once in jail, they had to pay steep fines to be released. Those who could not afford the fines were taken to the state of Yucatán to work off the debt laboring on public works projects.

The notorious episode was widely covered in the press, and was dubbed "The Dance of the Forty-One." Later it was discovered that one of the guests at the party had escaped arrest. Rumor had it he was the son-in-law of President Díaz and had been quietly let go. To this day, in Mexico the term "forty-one" is still used to refer to homosexuality.

Eight decades later, in the early 1980s, Alberto Mendoza, twelve or thirteen years old at the time, was riding in a car with his father. It was a hot summer day, and they were waiting to drive through the border checkpoint from Tijuana into San Diego, California. A commercial promoting San Diego's upcoming gay pride parade came on the radio. Alberto's father seethed, "They should set off a bomb and kill all those fags!" The comment deeply upset Alberto, who did not then openly identify as gay.

Twenty years after that, in 2013, Alberto decided to start an organization to claim his identity, for himself and for everyone else like him who had faced discrimination and bigotry because of their sexual orientation. He named it Honor 41.

Alberto Bartolomeo Mendoza was born in Ensenada, Baja California, Mexico. When he was less than a year old, his father, a salesman for Kirby vacuum cleaners, a popular brand at the time, was promoted and transferred to work in the company's Caribbean market, headquartered in Puerto Rico. For Alberto's father, who had grown up poor in a large family, this meant going from having practically nothing to suddenly entering a world of opportunity for his children. For almost ten years, the family lived in Puerto Rico, where Alberto's two younger brothers were born. Alberto was an outgoing, confident boy. Then the family relocated again, to the greater San Diego area in California.

"We lived three exits away from the border, but we went to Tijuana almost every day. My grandmother and aunts and uncles were there, and that's where I had my life. I decided I was a Mexican who slept in the United States. I grew up thinking my future could be in either country."

But the move did affect him, since Alberto's native language was Spanish and he could not talk easily in English with the other kids. This, coupled with the transition through puberty, made him more introverted and timid.

A few months after they moved, Alberto—tall, dark, and good-looking with a bright movie-star smile—found a way to make friends: there was a pool at his house, so he began inviting boys from school over. Happy to have friends, Alberto became a part of the group, and one of the boys started calling him "forty-one."

"I didn't know what it meant. To me, having a nickname meant I was one of them, because everybody had one—'Gordo,' 'Baldy,' whatever. I was really happy. But one day when we were all at my house, my dad came in and heard them calling me 'forty-one.' He called me out to the garage and asked me why they were calling me that. I told him it was my nickname. He said, 'They're calling you a faggot. Are you a faggot?'

"At that moment, I realized it was obvious to everyone. I knew I was different. I was more attracted to men than to women, and I had some feminine qualities. I wasn't necessarily a queen, but I wasn't typically masculine; it just wasn't me. I looked at my dad, and I told him no, I wasn't a faggot. He left the garage, kicked everyone out of the house, and told me I couldn't have them over anymore. After that, the other kids started taunting me, calling me 'forty-one' to make fun of me."

In spite of that painful incident, Alberto still didn't know why the number forty-one had anything to do with homosexuality. He reasoned that maybe in Mexico, if you still had not married and had children by the time you were forty-one years old, it was because you were gay. Satisfied with that explanation, he managed to push the matter aside.

When Alberto started tenth grade, he decided to run for vice president of his high school's student council. He spoke English very well by then, and wanted to find a way to fit in with the other kids. With a good instinct for human nature, he figured he would not win that year, but that through his campaign, the students would know his name and learn about his ideas. And that is what happened: he lost that year but entered the race again as a junior, and won.

Having a position of power at school opened up some other doors too. That is when Alberto's passion for activism began. He noticed that even though Latinos made up a majority of the student body, they were underrepresented in the school's extracurricular activities. Seventy percent of the students were Latino—half of them crossed the border from Mexico every day—and 20 percent were Filipino, but the latter group held most positions on the student council, on the cheerleading squad, on the baseball team, on the yearbook staff, on the student paper. With so many Mexican students, why don't we have anyone representing us? Alberto wondered. Then he had an idea: to get more Latino kids involved, information on extracurricular activities should be available in

English and in Spanish. Just a few weeks after joining the student council, Alberto proposed the creation of a Spanish-language student newspaper, *La Voz Azteca*.

Just as he began to feel secure socially again, another painful incident left a deep impression. At a monthly school assembly, while Alberto made a presentation, one of the students shouted "*Cuarenta y uno!*" (Forty-one!). Then other students joined in: "*Cuarenta y uno, cuarenta y uno, cuarenta y uno!*"

"I wanted to die. I wanted to disappear. Some kids knew what it meant, some didn't. To the teachers, it seemed like I was popular, but they were bullying me in front of everyone and I wanted to get out of there as fast as I could."

In an effort to leave the painful memory behind, Alberto transferred to another school the following year. He joined a fraternity, and when he was nineteen and fully aware of his homosexual identity, he went to a gay bar for the first time. He came out to his brothers at around the same time, and they were very understanding. Then he came out to his parents. To his surprise, his mother did not take it well, and that was hurtful to Alberto. It took a year before they were close again. His father's reaction surprised him too. He shook his son's hand and said, "Okay. I just hope you know how to defend yourself."

Even though he had come out to his family and felt comfortable with himself, the pain would return sometimes when he heard somebody say "forty-one," or when he heard derogatory comments about gay people.

"I didn't have any role models, a positive example to follow. At the time, the typical image of a gay person was Juan Gabriel or the drag queens, or hairdressers in feather boas, or men who you knew had sex with other men but they were married and stayed with their wives. There was no one in between who talked about being gay in a positive way. They were always criticized, made fun of, 'that fag.' When I started going out to the clubs in West Hollywood, there weren't any examples for me of what it meant to be a gay Latino man. As a gay man, the only role models were white men, even though I was a Latino man in my everyday life. I couldn't combine the two worlds. And when you met a Latino guy, he wasn't Marco anymore, he was Mark. Latinos had Americanized themselves because there weren't any other options."

Alberto believes that because of the lack of role models and his personal and professional development during those years, he became "adaptable, but also invisible." He learned how to look as good as any white man in a suit and tie, and how to show that he was well educated—he studied sociology and political science in college—with a large vocabulary, and he spoke without an accent. He learned how to be a Latino man who could fit in anywhere. But even so, there was no space where he could project himself as a successful gay man, because on top of the prevailing stereotypes, another stigma came along in the late eighties and early nineties for the gay community: the HIV and AIDS epidemic. Suddenly, any discussion of homosexuality quickly began to revolve around that issue.

HIV infection among the Latino community has especially concerned health-care officials because rates of infection have remained higher than in other ethnic or racial minority group ever since the disease was first discovered.

Although new diagnoses in the Latino community dropped by 4 percent between 2005 and 2014, diagnoses among gay and bisexual men in general rose by 24 percent, and diagnoses of young Latino gay and bisexual men between the ages of thirteen and twenty-four rose by 87 percent. In 2014, Latinos accounted for one-quarter of new HIV diagnoses (approximately 11,000 out of 45,000 new cases), even though Latinos only make up 17 percent of the general population in the United States. Seven of every ten Latinos diagnosed with the virus were gay or bisexual men, or had had sex with another man.[1]

The Centers for Disease Control at the US Department of Health has found there are cultural factors to explain the high numbers of Latinos infected with the virus, such as avoiding getting tested, seeking help, and getting treatment for fear of being discriminated against for being Latino. Machismo and the stigma around homosexuality in the Latino community play roles as do social factors such as poverty, migration patterns, low levels of education, a lack of access to health services, and language barriers. Immigration status can also be a consideration in seeking medical help: many undocumented Latino immigrants think that could result in the discovery of their immigration status, putting them at risk of deportation.

After graduating from college, Alberto worked at the Stop AIDS Project, an organization in San Francisco, as the coordinator of their Latino program. After that, he worked for a similar organization in Los Angeles, the AIDS Project, and got involved in other activist projects championing civil rights and environmental justice. Along the way he met many other Latino men, and found that they were always dealing with some kind of personal conflict: hiding their HIV-positive status, or hiding their sexual orientation from their parents or their employers. Alberto realized this put them at risk, with many of his friends turning to drugs or alcohol to ease the stress of hiding who they were; and at a certain point, that was no longer any fun.

In 2008, when Proposition 8, prohibiting same-sex marriage, was passed in California, Alberto once again wondered, "Where are the leaders in our community? Why are we not getting funding, why aren't we in positions of power? Where are the role models for young gay Latinos?"

Alberto would not start to find a way to answer those ever-present questions until 2012. Early that year, while talking with a close activist friend, Roland Palencia, Alberto mentioned that his birthday was coming up. He would turn forty-one, the number he hated so much because it had been used to bully him when he was in high school. Roland told him the story of the Dance of the Forty-One, and Alberto was stunned. He had never heard of it, and only then did he finally understand what that number really represented.

"The story made a huge impression on me, I could see myself in it. It made me so angry. For so long it had made me feel vulnerable, like it was a punishment. But now I know it wasn't a punishment. It was still in my consciousness because it was a part of my mission, and I had to understand it when I was ready to understand it, and open to doing what I had to do."

In the days following that revelatory conversation, Alberto remembers thinking about what he should do with the information he now had in his hands. He realized he did not want to start just another organization. He had to focus on what his community needed. He thought about how white men, when they come out of the closet, usually leave their families and move away to a city on the other side of the country, and start a whole new life, visiting their parents once or twice a year. Latinos don't do that. It's in their nature to be close to their families, talk to their parents, see how they're doing, and live near their siblings. Even so, it was hard for a family to accept a gay son. As Alberto saw it, this was a vicious circle: it's hard to share your own story when there aren't any other stories out there in the public sphere. He thought a change was not going to happen just because he wanted it to; he had to do something to make it happen.

"We have to celebrate ourselves in a different way, and I decided to do it through the story of the Forty-One, to honor those forty-one people who lost their lives by telling our stories: how we came out, our experiences with acceptance and rejection, how we deal with our families. Was it a fight? If not, how did they do it?"

Alberto started his project: he would publish a list of forty-one Latino people in the LGBTQ community with inspiring stories of struggle and perseverance. After coming up with the list, which included journalists, activists, politicians, artists, and business leaders, he produced short video biographies of each person to upload to the project's website. Honor 41 was born.

"I chose the name Honor 41, which you can say in English and Spanish, because for me this project is a reclaiming; it's a way to educate through the story," Alberto explains, four years after he first began publishing the annual list. "It says who we are and where we are. It's celebrating who we are and doing the best we can to help other young people who are having a hard time because of this."

On June 3, 2013, the day before his birthday and the last day he was forty-one, Alberto finished editing the last video of his first Honor 41 list.

Barack Obama is irritated. He had barely begun to deliver his prepared speech—eloquent and carefully worded, as usual—when a voice from the back of the room interrupts him, yelling, "President Obama! President Obama!" The shouts are heard off-camera. Obama, devoid of patience, raises his voice to cut off the unwelcome interruption.

"No! No, no, no, no, no! Listen, you're in my house. And you know what? It's a lack of respect when you're invited to someone's house . . ."[2]

The voice keeps shouting. Words can be heard alluding to undocumented immigrants, torture, and detention centers.

"You're not going to get a good answer if you interrupt me like this," Obama continues. "I'm sorry . . . no, no. You should be ashamed."

An exasperated Obama orders security to remove the interrupter from the room. He stops his speech celebrating LGBT Pride Month. It's Wednesday, June 24, 2015, at the annual gathering of leaders and activists of the LGBT community at the White House. This year, there is a special reason to celebrate: in just a few hours the Supreme Court will announce a historic ruling legalizing same-sex marriage. While the shouts continue, Obama tries to maintain his composure, but his expression is steely. He urges security to hurry up and escort the vocal protester from the East Wing of the White House.

Jennicet Gutiérrez, the protester in question, breaks out in an incredulous, mischievous smile as she recalls the episode. As an activist and a representative of the transgender community, she managed to get an invitation to the White House event and decided to take advantage of the opportunity to get out her message: immigration detention centers violate the rights of people like her. A week after the White House security team showed her the door, her life took a dramatic turn. She received many messages of support and solidarity, and some hateful ones too. But Jennicet, then twenty-nine and originally from Jalisco, Mexico, tried to focus on the positive ones, ignoring the negative. Today, sitting at a small table in the apartment she shares with a roommate in Van Nuys, an unremarkable neighborhood in northern Los Angeles, Jennicet gets emotional as she relives that special moment.

"I felt a strength inside me; it was fate. The White House has very strict access rules, so it was very meaningful that they gave that access to me, an undocumented, Mexican, transgender woman. I brought all the experiences I've lived through with me, and all my friends' pain, and listening to the president's speech, talking about all the progress the LGBTQ community has made, making everything sound so great, I snapped. I wasn't questioning that progress. I just wanted to point out a reality that my own community doesn't even want to see—the discrimination, the abuse my people are experiencing in the detention centers."[3]

Jennicet shouted at Obama that there cannot be progress for the LGBTQ community if one part of it—undocumented transgender women—continue to suffer discrimination. She yelled because she wanted to share the story of the seventy-five transgender people who sleep in detention centers every night, who are applying for political asylum, who are victims of violence. Ninety percent of them are women. But more than anything, Jennicet yelled at the president to reaffirm her own dignity as a woman.

"My name is Jennicet Gutiérrez. I am a proud undocumented transgender Latina," she announces in her profile video for Honor 41 in 2015. Jennicet has straight black hair, olive skin, and lively brown eyes. She explains, "My gender did not connect with my brain, so I started my process."

Getting to the point where she could proudly wear those three labels—Latina, trans, undocumented—has not been easy. Jennicet came to the United States fifteen years ago with her family. Of her siblings, she is the only one who is still undocumented. She has some happy memories from her childhood in Mexico, but she also remembers struggling to accept herself as she was. Migrating did not make things any easier. Being undocumented, not speaking the language, and the culture shock all made it hard to adapt to her new country. Jennicet tells me it took her ten years to find her voice.

It would not have been possible without the support of her family and the community that embraced her. She met Bambi Salcedo, a well-known transgender activist in Southern California and the president of the TransLatina Coalition. In 2014, Jennicet left her job at a hospital to work full-time as an activist for the group Familia: Trans Queer Liberation Movement.

According to that organization, the vulnerability of the transgender community in the United States remains an unresolved issue in the fight for LGBTQ rights. A study from the think tank Center for American Progress found that one of every three transgender people is a member of a racial minority group. But for undocumented transgender people, the figure is 98 percent.

"I want to show there is a violence connecting the minorities in this country, and a lot of people don't want to see those connections. They think since that person is African American, or gay, or transgender, it doesn't affect them," Jennicet explains. "I want people to see that connection, how the system keeps us divided."

Jennicet does not want to share the name on her birth certificate with me. "I think I have found that voice, and a lot of people identify with it," she says. "That's why I had the courage to go to the White House and confront the most powerful man in the world. I found the strength and courage to publicly denounce what my transgender sisters are going through. It was a big deal for me to say, 'I'm ready and I'm going to fight for my rights.'"

When Jennicet decided to spar with Obama, it wasn't an isolated impulse. A long history of allegations led up to her loud protest, which unintentionally turned into a battle cry covered by the media, with unexpected consequences. In November 2014, the investigation team at the Fusion television network, with funding from the Ford Foundation, published a report with statistics and personal stories from transgender women who had been victims of sexual abuse at immigration detention centers.[4] One out of every five hundred people detained in those centers is transgender. But one in five allegations of sexual abuse is from a transgender person. In these centers, detainees are housed in areas according to the information found in their personal identification. The problem is that many of these undocumented transgender women, fleeing violence in Central America and Mexico, have forms of identification that do not reflect their present gender identity.

The lack of documentation, therefore, becomes a problem that goes beyond the issue of migration: it reflects a lack of recognition of their true identity. Transgender women are housed with men, in settings where they are victims of physical, psychological, and sexual violence, and even torture.

"If you are undocumented, you can't finish the process of constructing your identity; it's all part of the same problem," Jennicet explains. "To change your name in the US, you have to have a Social Security number. If you're undocumented, you don't have one. Then you can't change your name. The only identification you have has the identity you were born with, which is not the one you identify with now. This causes legal and security problems. You can't identify yourself as the person you are trying to be."

One day, after the incident at the White House, a group of thirty-five Democratic congressional representatives sent a letter to Homeland Security secretary Jeh Johnson demanding the release of transgender women immigrants held in detention centers for men, because "these individuals are extremely vulnerable to abuse, including sexual assault, while they are in custody." Three days later, on June 29, Immigration and Customs Enforcement (ICE) released a memorandum with new guidelines establishing that, among other rules, people who identified as transgender would be housed in detention installations that correspond to their gender identity.

This was no doubt a nice, small victory for Jennicet and the LGBTQ movement, but no one let their guard down. If there is one thing activist groups have learned with Trump's rise to power, it is that things can always get worse. On November 15, 2017, a week after his presidential victory, three organizations led by the National Day Laborer Organizing Network met in Los Angeles to start working on a strategy of resistance to the new administration.

Jennicet was one of the speakers at the event. Later, at a press conference, she was clear: no matter who was in office, she would have done what she did, even though her four "labels"—undocumented, transgender, woman, Latina—made her vulnerable to the discrimination fomented by Trump's own rhetoric.

"Yes, I am scared. Yes, I am concerned. But fear is not going to hold me back," she said to a reporter from the *Advocate*, a magazine covering LGBTQ issues.[5] "If the media wasn't paying any attention to the issue of trans-women in detention centers, they definitely started to see it after the event with Obama. But with Trump in office, there will be many other issues needing our activism."

In 2015, the year Jennicet interrupted Obama, twenty-one transgender women were killed in the US.[6] In 2016, that figure rose to twenty-six.[7] Projections for the years to come are not at all optimistic.

Alberto smiles proudly when we talk about Jennicet. He also mentions Bamby Salcedo, founder of the TransLatin@ Coalition, who appeared on the Honor 41 list in 2013. The issue of representing diversity even within the LGBTQ movement was important to Alberto from day one—he did not want a list made up only of gay men.

"Most of them have had to come out twice, first as gay or lesbian and then as trans," Alberto explains. "They're at the bottom of the barrel, and I decided to include them from the beginning. I knew enough trans people to know their journey was harder than mine. The fact that sometimes they're forced to sell sex to survive, [that] they're more openly rejected, forces them into different closets."

The theme of two different closets also comes up when Alberto talks about "undocuqueers," part of the movement that developed in the fight to pass the DREAM Act, undocumented youth who found an opportunity to proudly claim their LGBTQ identity within the pro-immigrant cause, or vice versa. Alberto found that when he interviewed both trans people and Dreamers and asked them where they wanted to be in five years, it was hard for them to answer because of their uncertain immigration status. And some of the trans people even responded that they didn't know if they would be alive in five years.

Alberto also tried to include age diversity in Honor 41. He tried to find people from different walks of life: students, administrative assistants, activists, a senator, a judge. Thirty-five percent of the people who have been included on the list are HIV-positive, although some do not mention this in their interview. The hardest form of diversity to represent from a financial standpoint, because it would necessitate travel, was geographic. Alberto did not want to try to find corporate sponsors, which would imply some kind of obligation to them, so he decided to seek public donations. He applied for and received nonprofit status for his organization and included on the web page a request to donate $41 or more to the project. He produced the first video interviews with a digital camera, with somewhat crude sound quality. The first five people interviewed were activists David Damian Figueroa and Mario Guerrero; Alberto's friend, community leader Roland Palencia; actress and transgender activist Maria Roman; and police officer Candice Cobarrubias.[8] Of the 164 people interviewed for the project so far, 64 percent are of Mexican origin.

Imelda Plascencia and Claudia Iveth Ramirez share a video on the first Honor 41 list, and identify as queer and fluid. Imelda describes this as "looking beyond those binaries, not wanting to feel limited . . . wanting to just explore myself, and learn about others and the world that we live in in that process." They both work for the Collective of Immigrant Resilience through Community Led Empowerment (CIRCLE) Project and the Queer Dream Summer at UCLA's Dream Resource Center. Their work consists of creating spaces of healing justice for queer undocumented immigrants.

"We have conversations about our lives, about our families, about our experiences; we're very intentional about talking about why we're undocumented, why we continue to be undocumented, and you can't do that without talking about privilege, without talking about power dynamics, without talking about our society as a whole, and how it impacts us on a very personal and daily level," Imelda explains. "When you ask undocumented people where they're going to be in ten years, it brings up a lot of difficult feelings, difficult thoughts, because you're not guaranteed so many things, there's so much uncertainty. It's difficult to picture, even when you have something, it's difficult to enjoy because it can be taken away."

For Claudia, being undocumented and queer has been painful. She seeks to heal her own pain and help heal the pain of others through this project.

"My advice for anyone that's coming out is, find your community. Find people like you, people that will help you a lot, people that will uplift you. Oftentimes, it's really difficult to find a community, a queer community that's going to help you be a better person and help you move forward and heal. Oftentimes when we come out, you have to fit a role all the time. But you don't have to fit a role. Just be yourself."

Alberto goes on, "This project celebrates who we are, so that we can serve as role models, models that younger generations can follow, because I never had one. When I've invited people to participate, they're really enthusiastic. They just say yes right away without even seeing [the video]. It's strange for me to see that, now, people consider it an honor to be on the list. Now we've taken away the stigma and oppressive power associated with the number forty-one. These people live their lives outside of the closet and honor themselves, their families, and our community."

CHAPTER FIVE

SANCTUARY

Jeanette Vizguerra, forty-five
Mexico City/Denver, Colorado

IN HIS FIFTH DAY as president of the United States, Donald Trump signed an executive order to strengthen the application of immigration laws, and economically sanction city governments that failed to "employ all lawful means" to remove "aliens who had no right to be in the United States." This order was meant to punish so-called sanctuary cities. Although the order was blocked by a judge four months later, Trump succeeded in adding "sanctuary" to a growing list of polarizing issues in his five-day-old administration.

The sanctuary movement began in the United States over three decades ago. During the civil wars in Central America in the 1980s, thousands of Guatemalans and Salvadorans came to the United States to save their own lives. But they were not granted refugee status or asylum by the government. In response to their plight, an interreligious group came together to open the doors of its houses of worship and offer a safe haven for an indefinite time to people facing deportation, under the guise of "sanctuary." Those taking refuge inside the churches had the congregations' support.

Two decades later, in the wake of massive protests against anti-immigrant initiatives in 2006, the movement resurfaced. One of the recent cases is that of Jeanette Vizguerra, an undocumented immigrant who entered a church in Denver, Colorado, in February 2017 to avoid deportation. On April 20, after sixty-four days in sanctuary, Jeanette got a phone call: it was *Time* magazine, letting her know she had been named one of the 100 Most Influential People in the world.

Donald Trump was also on the list.

Jeanette Vizguerra has lived in the United States for twenty years. She and her family left Mexico City in 2007, fearing for their safety. Her husband, Salvador, was a driver for a public transportation company, and he had been the victim of two "express" kidnappings—where an immediate ransom is demanded for the victim's release, usually withdrawn from an ATM. He had been lucky, some of her husband's coworkers told him, because another driver had also been kidnapped and killed. When Salvador was kidnapped for a third time and survived, they decided to go to the United States. It was September, and Jeanette still had one semester to go before she would earn her degree in psychology.

Salvador went first, followed by Jeanette and their seven-year-old daughter three months later. They tried to cross the border near Las Cruces, New Mexico. Jeanette was detained there, and was back in Mexico that very day. Her daughter managed to keep going, along with the family friends who traveled with them. Fifteen days later, Jeanette tried to cross again, and this time she made it. On Christmas Day, the family was back together, ready to settle in Denver.

Jeanette told me she and her husband both got jobs. He worked as a manager for a moving company, and she did whatever work she could get. "Like everyone when they come here, it's the only way, with both working at whatever you can find."

I talked to Jeanette over the phone in late May 2017, twelve days after she returned home, after spending eighty-six days in sanctuary. As soon as she got out, Jeanette went back to her usual activities, including her activist work getting the word out about campaigns defending people who have been arrested by ICE and have valid arguments for why they should not be deported: they have never been convicted of a serious crime, they have lived in the country for many years, or they have small children who would suffer if the family were separated. Jeanette already had several years of experience as an activist even before she got involved with this issue, going back almost as long as she had been in the United States.

Her first job in the US was working for a cleaning company, an industry that employs many recent arrivals to the country. It did not take long for her to notice the injustices and abuses taking place in the company especially against workers without a work permit or regularized immigration status. She took it upon herself to review worker contracts and let other employees know whenever she discovered instances of wage theft or unfair firings.

Just seven months later, Jeanette was working at a local chapter of the Service Employees International Union (SEIU), one of the largest labor unions in the country. During her five-year tenure there, Jeanette specialized in defending civil rights and labor rights. She created a network of contacts across the whole country, and built alliances with other pro-immigrant social justice organizations. When she left the SEIU, she went to work at Rights for All People, a network of grassroots organizations working on a range of social justice issues including immigrant and worker rights. Jeanette worked there for thirteen years. In that time, she and her husband started their own cleaning company, bought a home, and had three more children. But they still had no way open to them to legalize their immigration status.

Then, on January 20, 2009, as Barack Obama began the first of two terms, Jeanette was pulled over for a minor traffic violation. She was found to be using a false Social Security number, and was taken to an immigrant detention center. For the next thirty-four days, Jeanette experienced firsthand what she had heard goes on inside those detention centers. She says the media was not covering what goes on in immigration detention at all at the time: the injustices, the mistreatment, the lack of medical attention, and how the suffering of people like her became a profitable business for a publicly traded corporation that derives its earnings from locking people up. The center where she was held in Colorado is managed by GEO Group, one of the largest private prison companies in the nation, which is awarded government contracts to operate them.

For every day an immigrant is held in one of their detention centers, GEO receives federal taxpayer money.

From inside, Jeanette could see what happened in there. She tells me, "I thought I had to do something, and that's when I decided to fight my case, and to do it publicly. I started talking about the injustices in the detention center, and everything you have to go through in there, and about the unfair laws that make you enter the system [Jeanette refers to immigrant detention centers as "the system"], and it really changes your life dramatically."

As part of the agreement with the prosecution for her release, Jeanette entered a guilty plea for using false documents. As a result of that plea, in 2011 she was issued an order of deportation. Then the appeals process began, which would go on for several years. It also marked the beginning of Jeanette's mission to share her story as widely as possible.

Jeanette was the first person in Colorado to make her detention and deportation story public. She tells me the English-language media never covered those cases, but she went out to speak at forums, in churches, and in schools. "I tried to raise people's consciousness, and they were sympathetic. They understood this was something that needed to be fought, that we could demand that laws like 287(g) [known as Secure Communities, an agreement between local and federal authorities stipulating that the former will perform immigration enforcement duties—an approach rejected and resisted by sanctuary cities] be repealed because they are restrictive and unnecessary; we already had secure communities."

Thanks to her lawyer's efforts, Jeanette was released from detention during the appeals process, on the condition that she attend regular check-in appointments with immigration authorities—these are generally scheduled every three months, every six months, or even once a year. At each check-in, the suspension of deportation was extended for the full period until the next scheduled appointment.

Jeanette showed up on time for every appointment. But in 2013, she got word from Mexico City that her mother was stricken with cancer. Jeanette was distraught. She faced the agonizing circumstance that sooner or later all undocumented immigrants in the United States face: a sick or dying mother, father, or sister needs them back home. What to do? Travel to be with them, even though returning to the US may not be possible? Find a "coyote" again, risk your life again, take the chance of being caught and put in detention again, leaving your own family behind in the US, not knowing for sure if you will ever see them again?

Jeanette made her decision. She would go to visit her mother in Mexico and come back to the US to be with her children however she could. But it was too late—Jeanette's mother died before she arrived, and Jeanette was only able to see her for the last time in a casket at the wake. The trip came at a very high price. Because she had left the country during her appeals process, the appeal was canceled. Under US immigration policy, anyone with an open appeal has to remain within US territory until it is completed, at a place where they can be located, for the duration of the process. This is part of the rationale for the check-in appointments. If Jeanette had managed to cross the border north undetected, the authorities might never have even known about her trip outside the country. But things did not go according to plan. When she tried to cross back into the US, Jeanette was arrested in El Paso, Texas, and transferred to a detention center in Denver, Colorado.

The battle to stay in the country started all over again. Drawing on resources she knew well from her years as an activist, and with her lawyer's support, Jeanette asked Colorado representatives in Congress to introduce a legislative initiative known as a "private bill," which aims to adjust the immigration status of a private individual or individuals, generally making an exception to a rule. Some private bills seek to suspend deportation orders on humanitarian grounds. This strategy worked, and Jeanette's deportation order was suspended for five months. After that, she was granted four extensions of the suspension, based on Jeanette's health and her children's emotional state. When a fifth extension was denied, Jeanette decided to take refuge in sanctuary.

Midway through our conversation, Jeanette seems a bit more relaxed. She tells me how, after her second stint in detention in

2013, she decided to start up the sanctuary movement in Denver. Since her case was not in court, Jeanette says she realized that she had to do something. There were sanctuary movements in other cities, so they could certainly build one right there in Denver. "I talked with my pastor, and asked her to put me in touch with the most progressive ministers and pastors," Jeanette said. "I explained the circumstances; she thought it was a good idea, and I started looking for people, for churches. For nine months, I spent every weekend going around with my children to talk to conservative churchgoers, to help them lose their prejudices and break taboos. I explained what creating a sanctuary meant; it's not just going to church and saying 'Let me in.' There are financial needs; there is a lot of preparation that needs to be done."

For nine months, Jeanette built a support network and worked on adapting a physical space as a shelter in the basement of her church, the First Unitarian Church of Denver—whose congregation of four hundred unanimously approved the project. In that time, she saw how the political climate in the US changed as Donald Trump was elected president and took office.

On February 8, 2017, Guadalupe García de Rayos, a Mexican woman who had lived in Arizona for over twenty years, became the first person to be deported by the Trump administration. Guadalupe's case was very similar to Jeanette's: Guadalupe had also had to appear regularly for check-in appointments with immigration authorities. But that day, when she arrived, ICE agents were already there waiting to arrest and deport her, even though Guadalupe had followed the protocol and the rules.

When Jeanette found out about Guadalupe, she made a decision. She was not going to give them the opportunity to make of her the next target for deportation. When the day of her next scheduled check-in came around, on February 15, she decided not to go. "I had the feeling I was going to be arrested. That's what was going to happen. I asked my lawyer to go for me and ask if they had the approval notice for my case [another deportation suspension], because they had been evaluating it for eighty-nine days.

It was a case they knew well for eight years by then, and I kept adding more evidence in my favor to it."

Hans Meyer, Jeanette's lawyer, and Ann Dunlap, her pastor, agreed to go to the immigration office as her representatives. If the document extending her deportation suspension was ready, then Jeanette would go to sign it. If it wasn't ready, she knew what she had to do.

As she waited for the news at home, where some reporters and cameramen familiar with her story were waiting with her, Jeanette got a text message from Dunlap: "Do not come here." Later Meyer called her to let her know the extension of the deportation suspension had been denied. A video shared on social media by Donie O'Sullivan, a producer for CNN, shows Jeanette breaking down in tears as she hears the news, while two of her daughters try to comfort her. In a press release, Jeanette said she knew she might have to spend all four years of Trump's term in sanctuary.

The basement space at First Unitarian that Jeanette had helped set up had already been occupied by Arturo Hernández García, another member of the community who was the first to benefit from Jeanette's initiative. Hernández García spent a few weeks in sanctuary, and was able to leave because his order of deportation was suspended. Jeanette's plan had worked. When her time came, everything was ready. Jeanette went into the church, spoke with the person in charge of communications, and said to let everyone know she was entering the church, and her reasons for doing so. Members of the press started to arrive within minutes. Her three months in sanctuary had begun.[1]

In the spring of 2006, large-scale protests took place in major cities including Chicago, New York, Phoenix, and Los Angeles, with hundreds of thousands marching through the streets, demanding respect for immigrant rights and urging Congress to pass immigration reform. This massive reaction, bringing out numbers of people never seen before—surpassed only by the Women's March, which took place in cities across the country the day after Trump's inauguration—was sparked by the December 2005 passage in the House of Representatives of the Border Protection, Antiterrorism, and Illegal Immigration Control Act, also known as the Sensenbrenner Bill, after the Republican congressman from Wisconsin who introduced it, Jim Sensenbrenner.[2] The bill did not pass the Senate, but it did reignite the pro-immigrant movement, while also inspiring a number of anti-immigrant legislative initiatives on the state level in the following years—the "Arizona Law" and the "Alabama Law," for example, which made it illegal to hire, rent a space, provide a service, or give aid of any kind to undocumented immigrants. It also reactivated the sanctuary movement through new interreligious coalitions that announced the doors of their houses of worship were open, just as they had been in the 1980s. Cases like that of Elvira Arellano, an undocumented immigrant originally from Michoacán, Mexico, who remained in sanctuary in a Chicago church for an entire year, kept appearing in national and international media.

Although the whereabouts of immigrants in sanctuary is publicly known, immigration authorities have not yet dared to enter a church by force to remove someone and have them deported. This policy was reaffirmed in the document known as the Morton Memo, sent out in 2011 by the director of Immigration and Customs Enforcement (ICE), John Morton, instructing immigration agents to follow the guidelines established by the Obama administration and prioritize the arrest of criminals or people who posed a national security risk. The memo advised agents to avoid "sensitive" places, including churches, hospitals, and schools.[3]

As we know, in spite of Donald Trump's openly anti-immigrant rhetoric, his predecessor in the White House earned the distinction of being responsible for more deportations than any other president in US history. Barack Obama closed out his eight years in office with over three million deportations to his credit,[4] and of those, two million were Mexicans.[5] The difference is that under the Obama administration, there still existed the possibility of a negotiated deal on immigration reform, with the sanctuary movement functioning as a parallel strategy. Under the Trump administration, for some, sanctuary is the only option.

This could help explain the rise in the number of faith organizations that have declared themselves as sanctuary. In 2014, 250 congregations, including synagogues, had joined the movement. After the immigration raids of January 2016, that number grew to 400 congregations.[6] By November of that year, when Trump won the presidential election, the figure had doubled, to 800. The Department of Homeland Security (DHS) website still characterizes houses of worship as sensitive locations, but people working with the undocumented community see no reason to believe this policy could not change under the Trump administration.

It is hard to calculate the number of undocumented people actually living in sanctuary at any given time, partly because many of them want to keep their cases as private as possible, out of fear of deportation. Generally, the ones who are vocal and public about their cases tend to be people who have been involved with activism for many years, like Jeanette.

In some of the so-called sanctuary cities, local police officers, responsible for maintaining order, or sheriff's officers, who operate in counties, refuse to arrest people simply because of their immigration status.

According to law, federal agents should seek the support of local police to make arrests in cases where immigration rules have been violated; but the law does not require local officers to arrest undocumented immigrants solely because their federal counterparts request it, unless a crime has been or may have been committed in their local jurisdiction. When cases on this issue have reached federal courts, judges have ruled that complying with a federal request is at the discretion of local agencies.

The main reason police or sheriff's officers in various states refuse to cooperate with Secure Communities, say many politicians and activists, is that if any interaction with the police may result in a deportation, undocumented communities will be even more marginalized and isolated than they already are. Many undocumented immigrants fear that coming into contact with law enforcement will mean their immigration status will be discovered and they could be arrested and deported. As a result, when they are victims of or witnesses to a crime, such as robbery, assault, extortion, workplace abuse, and domestic or gender-based violence, they may be reluctant to come forward or press charges. This generates a cycle of constant vulnerability.

Compounding the fears based on immigration status is the fact that in the United States, as demonstrated by statistical data, ethnic minorities, especially African Americans and Latinos, are arrested at higher rates and receive more severe sentences than a comparable proportion of whites committing the same levels of crimes.[7] "Racial profiling," the practice of stopping someone solely based on their physical appearance, has been denounced for years by human rights and activist organizations. One well-known experiment, in which subjects see a white man trying to open a car door in a parking lot with a coat hanger and a black man doing the same, showed that many assumed the white man lost his keys and that the black man was trying to steal the car.[8]

For years, state and local governments have launched campaigns to counter this perception and incentivize racial and ethnic minorities to come forward when they have been victims of crimes, under the premise that no one has to ask about a victim's immigration status or criminal record when a crime is reported or in order to press charges. In cities including Los Angeles, San Francisco, and New York, which have openly declared themselves sanctuary cities, police departments conduct frequent training sessions with the aim of building trust in law enforcement among undocumented communities. If those police in sanctuary cities signed on to the Secure Communities program, all the gains they have made gaining confidence would instantly erode.

Trump's proposal to freeze federal funding for sanctuary cities was blocked in court—like some of his other executive orders—because, based on a previous Supreme Court ruling, such a measure would only be justified when it represents a "federal interest" greater than the issue at hand. Cities, counties, and states with sanctuary policies receive federal money from dozens of departments and administrations, but most of those agencies have nothing to do with immigration control. Also, federal funding does not necessarily cover a significant amount of a city's budget. For example, in New York City, federal funds represent only 10 percent of the city's budget, which was $80 billion in 2015.

An analysis by the *Washington Post* found that many counties with sanctuary policies receive very little or almost no funds from federal Justice Department programs, which could constitute a "federal interest" warranting the withholding of resources to those counties: of the $165 million allocated from the Justice Department, only $18 million go to jurisdictions with noncooperation policies with immigration authorities.[9]

Some cities and counties have implemented policies that go further than refusing to arrest undocumented immigrants solely because of their immigration status. California has authorized issuing driver's licenses to undocumented people and offers interpretation services in several languages at local government offices. The District of Columbia recently set up a legal defense fund for undocumented immigrants; deportation proceedings take place in civil court instead of criminal court, facilitating the defendant's access to a defense attorney, which is not a consideration in immigration cases in criminal court.

In the First Unitarian Church basement, as the days passed, the yellow walls gradually became covered over with posters activists had made to keep up Jeanette's spirits, and with children's drawings from the times her children and grandchildren came to visit. Photos taken of the living space there over the course of Jeanette's three months in sanctuary show notebooks and colored pencils for drawing, a microwave, cleaning products, a small space heater, and a rosary on the wall.

In an interview with a television reporter, Jeanette, in tears, explains her reasons for voluntarily entering the church: "My kids are my life; my family is my life. *No es* my country, *pero es* my house, the house of my kids, and the country of my kids. I'm living more years here than in my country."

When Jeanette arrived in the United States, her daughter Tania was seven years old. Now she is twenty-seven and a beneficiary of the Deferred Action for Childhood Arrivals, or DACA, the program of temporary protection implemented in 2012 by Barack Obama, for young people who arrived in the country undocumented as minors. Jeanette's other three children are US citizens: Luna, thirteen; Roberto, ten; and Zury, six. She also has three grandchildren.

"I think I've done a good job with them," Jeanette says modestly but firmly when we talk about her kids. In almost every interview of her that I've watched or listened to, Jeanette's voice breaks a little when the subject turns to her children. This time is no exception. She explains that her studies in psychology helped her to understand it's important to be honest with children about what's happening. It's a mistake to think they won't understand just because they're children. "They have all been activists right along with me; all four understand how things are and why we have to fight. When I decided I would go into sanctuary, my children told me they would be my voice on the outside."

That could have been just a nice thing to say, but Jeanette's children really did speak out on her behalf. On April 13, 2017, while Jeanette was in the church basement, her children traveled to Washington, DC, as part of the "Caravana de niños," or Kids Caravan, a national action where dozens of children of undocumented parents, or parents who have been deported or have orders of deportation, tried to soften Trump's heart and affirm their right to have their parents with them in the country of their birth.[10]

Jeanette tells me that children who, along with their families, experience the fight to defend their family's rights and try to change the laws are affected too. "They grow up before their time, their intellectual development is not the same as other children's; they use language different from a typical child. My son Roberto says he's thinking about being the president, because these unfair laws have to change."

Along with her family's love and support, Jeanette had the strong support of her community. Clearly moved, she tells me about all the expressions of love and solidarity people sent her throughout her time in sanctuary. She received messages from all across the country and gifts to make her stay in the basement more comfortable. People sent supermarket gift cards for her children so they would not have to go without anything. During those three months, Jeanette continued giving workshops and presentations remotely. She came up with a security plan in case it was necessary to leave quickly. Even though an immigration agent had never before entered a sanctuary space, Jeanette believes the Trump administration has no respect for anything, so she decided it was best to be prepared.

Jeanette's experience with the media was very positive during this time. Her story was told in local and national outlets, and also internationally in the press in Japan, China, and France, and through Skype interviews in Mexico and elsewhere in Latin America.

"I got a lot of attention," she says, "because ever since Trump, migration was getting talked about more. It was about time the subject got the attention it needed, and I'm happy my case helped with that. I've always known this is a double-edged sword, and my public profile could get me thrown out quicker, or it could help make a change."

But Jeanette never imagined just how public her profile was about to get. She had been living in the church basement for almost two months when she got a phone call from her lawyer's office. What she was told sounded like some kind of joke.

"Jeanette, I've got news. You have been nominated as one of the 100 Most Influential People by *Time* magazine," an assistant of Meyer's told her, explaining the final list would be published April 20.

Jeanette did not take this very seriously. But a week later, she received in the mail the formal invitation to attend the gala celebrating the winners at Lincoln Center, in New York City. Then Jeanette saw that she had been included in a list alongside President Donald Trump, his daughter Ivanka, and his son-in-law, Jared Kushner.

"Just imagine, twenty years of my life doing so many things, fighting. Yes, I did feel the satisfaction of knowing I have made a difference," Jeanette says without false modesty. "Here in Colorado, I have built a community; my voice is heard. And it made me proud to be able to say: 'Trump, I am shutting you up. We are not criminals; we can be right on the same list as you. And I can enjoy this award because my people respect and appreciate me. Three-quarters of the country hate you.' How can that man sleep at night, knowing children are being left without mothers and fathers because of a deportation?"

On April 20, at five o'clock in the morning, Jeanette got the news that she had made the final list. She had spent sixty-four nights in sanctuary. She asked that her children be brought over. A few hours later, dressed in black pants, a black blouse with white dots, and a lightweight white sweater, her hair down in loose curls framing her dark face, with sharp features and small eyes, she emerged on the church front steps. Jennifer Piper, director of the interreligious program of the American Friends Service Committee, the organization behind the "Sanctuary Everywhere" campaign, stood alongside Jeanette and First Unitarian's pastor, Mike Morran.[11]

Addressing the crowd that had gathered, Pastor Morran said that as people of faith, they were called to defend the families who are the base of their life in common. He emphasized that even though we may call God by different names, we are all called to work together against senseless forces trying to separate a mother from her children. Turning to Jeanette on the steps, he said, "This faith community believes separating this family is a great injustice."

With Piper serving as interpreter, Jeanette stood before the microphones and began speaking in Spanish. She explained that for her, this acknowledgment came after twenty years of struggle, of forging a path. She spoke about the fear, anger, and deception that come from living with the knowledge that governments are trying to break up families. She said she shared the honor with all migrant families fighting like her and also said that this fight is not only to keep families together, it's a fight against hate. Her voice breaking from emotion, Jeanette dedicated the award to her children, at her side. She thanked the congressmen who had tried to find alternatives so she could stay in her community in an effort to show "we are not criminals."

Referring to one of her fellow Most Influential People, Jeanette said, "I have contributed to this country with twenty years of hard work, and all those years I have paid taxes, and I can prove it, unlike Mr. Trump, who has not produced his tax return. We immigrants are not criminals; we are productive people." Jeanette, of course, could not attend the gala in New York. She had her own celebration, surrounded by the people she loves, in sanctuary, with her community.

Right on the heels of the *Time* list, Jeanette got more good news: on May 12, immigration authorities informed her lawyer that a private motion presented by Colorado senator Michael Bennet on her behalf had been accepted, along with thirty-two similar initiatives that had been presented from around the country before May 5. Through an email, they were notified that for these thirty-two cases in particular, the criteria to suspend the order of deportation as applied by the Obama administration would be respected, while noting that future cases would not be treated in the same way. By then, Jeanette had moved to First Baptist Church, because some remodeling work was taking place at First Unitarian.

When she got the news, Jeanette decided to make it public through a live broadcast on her Facebook page. With her hair pulled back and a huge smile on her face, accompanied by a few others in a small room, Jeanette started to talk in a voice that sometimes faltered with emotion. She thanked everyone who had made it possible for her to stay in the country, from her lawyer to those who opened the doors of their churches.

"Tomorrow, I am leaving sanctuary. We did it! Tomorrow I'm leaving the church. I can be with my family. . . ." Jeanette's voice breaks. She pauses to compose herself, but she cannot hold back her tears. "This is one of the best Mother's Days. I can be with my children in my house. . . . I want to thank the churches that have welcomed us, that have given us the safe space to resist our deportation processes. To my children, my grandchildren . . ." Her voice catches in her throat again; she pauses for a moment. "To my father, who always gave me strength from Mexico, saying, 'Daughter, don't give up.'"

The new suspension of her deportation order, in effect for two years, was made possible in part because of the support Jeanette received from federal, state, and local officials, as well as the private motions presented by Senator Michael Bennet and Colorado congressmen Jared Polis and Ed Perlmutter. But Jeanette has another legal process in motion. In 2016, she applied for a U visa, which is given to people who have been the victims of a crime. Several years earlier, Jeanette had accused her husband of physically attacking her. Although, according to Jeanette, this was an isolated incident, if she gets the visa, her order of deportation will be permanently suspended and she will be allowed to live in the US for at least three years. Jeanette and her husband are now separated, but on good terms.

The day Jeanette and I talked on the phone, the proposed federal budget for 2018 was revealed. No budgetary cuts for sanctuary cities were in it. Even so, Jeanette is uneasy. She is sure the Trump administration will find another way to "suffocate" people trying to support immigrants, or those who simply refuse to carry out immigration enforcement tasks that are not their responsibility.

"I want our communities to be stronger. I want to be with my family, with my children. And I want more equality for everyone in the world; I want people to be respected no matter their race or origin. But the immigration fight is not going to stop, no matter what. My grandfather was part of the Bracero Program, and he died in that program. This is a long-term fight."

The film and Emmy-winning actress, producer, and activist America Ferrera wrote the small biography of Jeanette Vizguerra published in *Time* magazine.[12] It read,

> Some families have emergency plans for fires, earthquakes or tornadoes. Jeanette Vizguerra's family had an emergency plan for a dreaded knock at the door. If US Immigration and Customs Enforcement officials came to her home, her children knew to

film the encounter, alert friends and family and hide in the bedroom. The Vizguerra family lived in terror of being ripped apart by deportation.

Ferrera describes Vizguerra's work as an outspoken advocate for immigration reform as "a bold and risky thing for an undocumented immigrant" and ends with, "She shed blood, sweat and tears to become a business owner, striving to give her children more opportunities than she had. This is not a crime. This is the American Dream."

CHAPTER SIX

A LIFE LIVED WITHIN TWENTY-NINE MILES

Mónica Robles, forty-two
Nogales, Sonora/Río Rico, Arizona

NIGHTS IN ARIZONA CAN SEEM TIMELESS. Outside the few big cities in the state, like Phoenix or Tucson, Arizona nights are all desert and starry sky. The little towns, some with little patches of green, others completely arid, can barely be made out in the darkness, from the faint glow of scattered streetlights and the few businesses open late. But out on the highway, as you gaze up, the sky is a great starry blanket nestled over the small towns out in the middle of nowhere, just as it was twenty years ago, or forty, or more.

Rio Rico is one of those towns. Located twenty minutes north of the border separating the two cities named Nogales, one in Mexico and one in Arizona, Rio Rico has 19,000 inhabitants, 16,000 of whom are Latinos in a state where one of every twenty residents is undocumented.[1]

Travelers headed north from the border drive along Interstate 19, a highway sixty miles long that ends in Tucson, where it runs into Interstate 10, one of the longest highways in the country. Undocumented people cannot venture farther than Tubac, a little town fourteen miles north of Rio Rico and twenty-nine miles north of "the line." There, a permanent immigration checkpoint has become a second border. People who have crossed the first border without papers tend to live trapped in a tiny subcountry, twenty-nine miles wide, between two immigration checkpoints.

Mónica Robles is one of those people.

Mónica is forty-two years old, and for eighteen years she has lived within this twenty-nine-mile strip. Born in Nogales, Mexico, she lived there until just before her twenty-fifth birthday. She arrived in the US with a temporary visitor visa, the same one that almost everyone living along the border has. Her mother was a US citizen and lived on the northern side of the border. Mónica's three children, twin girls and a boy, were born in the United States, something they are grateful for because "there's no future for them in Mexico." Mónica wanted her daughters to go to school in Arizona, so the family moved there.

When Mónica started living in the United States, the challenge was to find a job without a work visa. She began cleaning houses and making cakes to sell at the open-air market. First she and her family lived in an apartment, and then her mother bought a house in the highlands of Rio Rico, up in the mountains, and they all moved in.

"My mother told me, 'This house is for you and my grandchildren. I want them to be in a better place.' She bought the house with a loan in 2007, and that same year she bought a car, maroon. It's the one I still drive; it's pretty beat up," Mónica says, gesturing out the window toward the car.

We're sitting in her living room, with brightly colored walls, big comfy chairs, and an atmosphere filled with the warmth of family. It's Saturday, in the evening, and the land out in front of her house is covered in the darkness of the mountains, a few stars sparkling in the night sky. Mónica, pretty with a light-brown complexion and reddish dark hair that falls around her jaw, wears a bright red jacket that matches her lipstick.

The year 2007 was a good one for the family, but their luck did not last long. In October, Mónica's mother was diagnosed with pancreatic cancer, a devastating disease that often kills very quickly, but in this case it meant a long three-year battle. Mónica, who was pregnant with her third child at the time, took care of her mother and worked making tamales to sell to bring in some income; her mother's Social Security check barely covered the mortgage pay-

ment. There's a saying, "One tragedy never comes alone," and for
Mónica that proved to be all too true. A few months before her
mother died, the father of her first two children, who lived in Mexico and provided financial support for his kids, was killed.

"There were a lot of murders happening then and he was shot
in a bar. My mother cried a lot; she worried about what would
happen to us after she died. I told her, 'Don't cry. I'm not helpless.
I'm not just going to sit around. If you need to go, go in peace.' At
first I prayed she wouldn't die, but after watching her suffer, I said,
'God, please take her. I can't see her like this.'"

Mónica's mother died in 2011, and by then the father of her
youngest child had also died from surgery complications. Mónica
was left alone with her three children, with no financial help, undocumented, and with a mortgage to pay. For a year she worked
babysitting, selling clothes, and making tamales three or four days
a week, but she still could not keep up payments on the house. She
tried to work something out with the bank, but her negotiation efforts went nowhere, and she eventually received an order to vacate
the premises.

"I lived like that for a year; it was horrible. I would go to bed
and couldn't sleep, worrying about how they were going to throw
me out of the house. What could I do? Where could I go with my
kids? It was a constant fear. Until one day, I decided not to cry
anymore. You fight so hard for things. You get sick like my mother
did. You die, and in the end you can't take anything with you. I had
high blood pressure, and I couldn't sleep, so I told myself I had to
calm down."

After coming to terms with the loss of her mother's house,
Mónica decided to look for some other kind of work besides babysitting, which was her main source of income. That's how her full-
time business preparing food started.

In the United States and almost every country, informal employment tends to be ignored, "unseen" from a public-policy perspective. When it is recognized, it tends to be criminalized, part of the
"black market" undertaken by undocumented migrants or tax evad-
ers. Nevertheless, beyond these stereotypes, this kind of work allows

families with small businesses to stay afloat, even in times of financial crisis, or especially during those times. Many young people, regardless of immigration status, start out working as babysitters or mowing lawns, cleaning houses or preparing food to sell. And many people also supplement their income from steady jobs with work in the informal economy, with its flexible hours.

A poll conducted by the Federal Reserve Bank of Boston in 2014 determined that the informal-work participation rates among four employment status groups were as follows: 42.8 percent of full-time workers, 59.4 percent of part-time workers, 39.6 percent of people seeking a job, and 26.5 percent of those classified as "other" or "not working." In total, around 44 percent of survey respondents reported participating in some informal paid work during 2011–13 to supplement their primary income. One of every four people classified as "not participating in the work force" by the Bureau of Labor Statistics had some kind of informal job.[2]

Mónica belongs to this last group. Before her mother got sick, she had sold food with a friend, and it had gone pretty well. With her mother's illness and the birth of her third child, she stopped. But four years later, Mónica took it up again. She began preparing around fifteen or twenty meals for local workplaces, and sold around half of those. She offered her food for sale directly, unabashed. Now she delivers and sells around sixty or seventy meals a day.

Mónica lights up as she tells me this. She smiles brightly, her big eyes gazing skyward in amazement. She remembers cooking in the tiny apartment she went to live in after her mother passed away, then packing up the food, loading it in her car, and going out to sell it. She doesn't have to do that anymore. Now she sells meals to the staff at four schools and a few other businesses, "all very professional people," she adds. Every morning she brings around the day's menu and takes down their orders. And not only that, she has become a job creator, paying two people to work for her. Her son also helps out with the deliveries.

"You wouldn't believe how crazy my life is," she says, trying to be very serious, but she can't help but break out in a proud smile again. "Every night I'm in the kitchen, I go to bed at one or two in the morning, I get up at six, drop my son off at school, come back and just cook, clean the kitchen, shop for the next day. And then it depends on what dish I'm making. If I'm going to make chiles rellenos, I make around eighty or a hundred; if I'm making roast beef, that's around twenty or thirty pounds of meat—and then out to make deliveries. Where I go, they all know me by now. But it's a constant struggle," she says of her daily routine to make ends meet.

I first heard about Mónica from Julio Sánchez, a fellow journalist who works near the border. We met in February 2017 at an event in Nogales, Mexico, and we talked about how migration policies could become harsher under Trump's administration. Our conversation turned to the twenty-nine-mile strip, one of the narrowest stretches between border security checkpoints in the country.

These inner tiers of security along the borders and coastal areas of the United States follow a policy established by the Department of Justice in 1953. Without ever coming up for public debate or consideration, a one-hundred-mile border zone was established around the entire continental US, as well as Alaska and Hawaii, under the jurisdiction of the Department of Homeland Security, through Customs and Border Protection (CBP), which oversees the Border Patrol. There were fewer than 1,100 Border Patrol agents at that time; now there are more than 21,000. The Trump administration's former head of the Department of Homeland Security, John Kelly, announced that 15,000 more agents would be hired.[3]

It is widely assumed that border and immigration politics only affect people who live in border cities such as El Paso, Texas, and San Diego, California. But Border Patrol operations extend around the whole country: roughly two-thirds of the US population, or two hundred million people, live within the hundred-mile zone. Most or all of the areas of Florida, Hawaii, Massachusetts, New Jersey, and New York lie within the hundred-mile strip. Nine out of ten of the largest metropolitan areas in the country are located within that zone: New York City, Los Angeles, Chicago, Houston, Philadelphia, Phoenix, San Antonio, San Diego, and San Jose.

According to the CBP website, there are 145 Border Patrol stations within the hundred-mile zone.[4] Texas has the most, with 54, followed by California and Arizona. Although the CBP only lists 45 permanent checkpoints on interstate highways or other heavily trafficked roads, there are dozens of other "tactical" checkpoints operated by the same agency. Some organizations have identified up to 200 of these in different areas.[5]

The permanent checkpoint on Interstate 19 is in the northern area of the small town of Tubac. As with all checkpoints of this kind, drivers have to slow down as they approach the checkpoint and follow the agents' instructions. Generally, US citizens just have to answer "yes" when the agent asks if they are citizens, and they'll be on their way. Visitors must show their immigration documents. Up until several years ago, those in Mónica's situation could take the risk crossing through the checkpoint by simply saying they were citizens. But with stricter application of immigration laws in the wake of the September 11, 2001, terrorist attacks, agents exercise greater scrutiny at checkpoints, and anyone found to be lying to an immigration official could be charged with a federal crime. So now, undocumented immigrants living between checkpoints are trapped: they cannot travel into the country's interior for fear of being questioned about their immigration status, which could result in their arrest and deportation, and they can't venture outside the US because they won't be allowed back. They live in a narrowly defined limbo.

The Fourth Amendment to the US Constitution protects citizens from unreasonable searches and seizures. But the American Civil Liberties Union, the most important organization defending civil rights in this country, has received hundreds of complaints of constitutional rights violations during these "routine" checks. In 2014, the ACLU sued the government on behalf of fifteen citizens who claimed they had been unjustly harassed at checkpoints. Hundreds more have uploaded videos on the internet showing how Border Patrol agents abused them or harassed others at these checkpoints.

At ports of entry along the border, federal authorities do not need an order or even a reasonable suspicion to justify these routine checks, which may include thorough vehicle searches. In the first months of the Trump administration, searching through people's cell phones, which generated some controversy, brought this issue to the forefront. But these checks don't happen only at the border, they are also carried out at any point within the hundred-mile zone, which, according to the ACLU, constitutes an "extra-constitutional" power.

According to Border Patrol regulations, agents cannot detain anyone without a "reasonable doubt" that the person has violated immigration law or committed a crime. And they cannot search vehicles without a warrant or "probable cause," which means a reasonable suspicion based on actions and circumstances that a violation of immigration law or a crime has been committed. But in practice, Border Patrol agents "routinely ignore or misunderstand the limits of their legal authority in the course of individual stops, resulting in violations of the constitutional rights of innocent people," according to an ACLU report on the subject.[6] These overreaches of authority occur due to a lack of adequate training for agents, inadequate supervision from Homeland Security authorities, and a lack of sanctions imposed by CBP on agents that abuse their authority.

"The federal government's dragnet approach to law enforcement and national security is one that is increasingly turning us all into suspects," the ACLU report concludes. "If Americans do not continue to challenge the expansion of federal power over the individual, we risk forfeiting the fundamental rights and freedoms that we inherited—including the right to simply go about our business free from government interference, harassment and abuse."

Aside from what people passing through the checkpoints experience, activists and authorities have denounced other impacts of the installation and operation of these points. Along the border with Mexico, they tend to be located on the only existing passable roads, surrounded by ranches, motion detectors, and harsh terrain. In Arizona and Texas, there are some points that are strongly monitored inside the strip between checkpoints. In Texas, there have been documented cases of agents stopping ambulances to check the immigration status of patients. In 2015, the *New York Times* reported an account of a Brownsville pediatrician who stated that a child had died en route to Corpus Christi and the parents had not accompanied him because they were undocumented and were afraid to cross through the checkpoint. Officials in Brooks County, which has a checkpoint in Falfurrias, Texas, have reported finding almost five hundred dead bodies since 2009.[7] Local activists believe they were immigrants who have died of heat exhaustion trying to circumvent the checkpoint—temperatures rise above one hundred degrees there in the summer.

"You think you can't go to the other side now, but someday you will be able to. You don't have any choice but to put up with it," Mónica tells me when our conversation turns to the limitations imposed on her by the checkpoint. "I have been about to cross it, and then I think: No, I can't risk what I have. When my mom was in the hospital, she was in Tucson, on the other side of Tubac, and I thought, 'How can I get there?' Because it's really tricky; you can't. I had to stay here; my brothers went. But you have to imagine someday you could or you'll go crazy."

One of my first assignments as a reporter for the daily *La Opinión* in Los Angeles was to do a story on a "Raza Graduation" at a university in San Diego, just north of Tijuana, Mexico. Some colleges with high percentages of Latino students, primarily from Mexico, celebrate Raza graduations every year. At these events, held separately from official graduation ceremonies, graduates attend with members of their family or close friends. In a warm, intimate atmosphere punctuated with cultural elements from their native countries, the students express their gratitude to their parents and others for all the support and love they got during their years in school.

This ceremony has a special meaning, because for many Latino students, just getting to college represents a major challenge. In the United States, the costs of higher education are extremely high, and students who do not have the financial means to pay apply for financial aid in the form of loans and scholarships from state and federal governments. But undocumented students without Social Security numbers are ineligible for financial aid. If they want to earn a degree, they have to pay the same tuition foreign students pay, which is the highest of all. Those who pursue a higher education in spite of the challenges are able to do so thanks to enormous personal and family sacrifices; everyone helps out so the student can go to school. That is the essence of the Raza Graduation: giving thanks for the extraordinary efforts their families have made so that the student could get to where they are, so they can in turn help out those following in their wake.

On the day of my first Raza Graduation, I arrived in the meeting room where about thirty families were gathered to celebrate with their graduates. It was a beautiful ritual: a professor announced the names of graduates and, wearing a graduation cap and gown, they would take the stage accompanied by their parents, or a sibling or other family member. There on the stage, the graduate introduced family members to the audience and said a few words of thanks to them, generally mentioning the money to pay for tuition and books, and the Tupperware containers of beans taken back to school after weekend visits home. Instead of the graduate receiving a diploma, in this ceremony, the families received recognition and applause. The families left the stage beaming with pride and emotion.

Then it was time for a young man named Mario to take the stage. To my surprise, unlike the students before him who had been accompanied by mothers, fathers, siblings, and grandmothers, Mario went up alone. Wearing his cap and gown, Mario said he was there that night to thank the people who had made it possible for him to make it to graduation, but, paradoxically, they could not be there with him. He said that some of his friends had offered to go with him when they heard about his situation, but he chose to go alone so that he could tell his story.

Mario's parents were undocumented and lived in Los Angeles, two hours north of San Diego. To travel south to San Diego and north again, you have to go through a checkpoint in San Clemente, seventy miles north of the border. Mario's parents could have gone to San Diego to be there with him and bask in their son's praise and the warm recognition of the other families present. But they would have run the risk of getting stopped by immigration agents on the way back. The celebration might have ended in a deportation.

Mario started telling this story with a lump in his throat, struggling to keep his emotion under control, until he let out a cathartic sob. He told the audience how when he was a little boy he had hated his father because he was never home, and he had held down two jobs and had no time to spend with his children. But, now, Mario explained, he knew it was thanks to his father's hard work, as well as his mother's and sister's, that he was able to graduate with a degree in engineering. He also said that even though he had accomplished his goal that day, he would not be able to get a job in the profession he had worked so hard and sacrificed so much to join since he lacked papers to work legally in the United States. Mario finished his speech, wiped away his tears, and left the stage.

If Mexican immigrants have one thing in common, it's the hope that their children will have a better life. After covering immigration in the United States for years, I've found that seems to be the constant defining those who come here. As Mónica says, it's a never-ending struggle, but it will be worth it because her children will be better off.

Mónica's two eldest daughters are twins, twenty-one years old. For the past three years they have lived in Tucson, where Interstate 19 meets Interstate 10. Because of the checkpoint, Mónica cannot visit them. Her daughters both work full-time and attend college. Mónica helps them out financially, pays for their health insurance, and often cooks for them.

"I freeze everything. Whenever they come here I have their containers of frozen food ready so they don't have to cook, because sometimes we don't see each other, we're not here at the same time. And I tell them, 'Study hard, because you have the opportunity.' I studied business administration, but I left after five semesters, I didn't finish my degree. I tell them, 'If you don't want to end up like me, cooking and scrubbing . . .' Look, I'm all burned"—she shows me her hands, her forearms—"I burned myself with the beans; they were boiling, and I spilled the oil. I make good money, thank God, even more than some people who have papers and college degrees. The problem is, I can't save anything, because everything I make goes to rent, the electric bill, other bills. And I know I'm not supposed to be doing this, because I don't have a license to sell food, but I have God's permission, and I pray that the police don't stop me and that I stay healthy. I say to God, 'You know what I need; protect me, and I'll take care of everything else.'"

Since her daughters are US citizens and over twenty-one, the age that citizens can legally petition for legal residency for their parents, Mónica's situation could change for the better in the years to come. Then she would be free to come and go anywhere within the country and outside it. And perhaps one day she may be able to attend her daughters' graduations in Tucson.

As we reached the end of our conversation, inevitably we touched on the topic everyone brings up when discussing immigration these days: the policies of Donald Trump's administration.

"He has no fear of God, that shameless bastard," Mónica says with a loud laugh. "There are people who hurt other people so much, and they're not afraid of anybody but fear God, because He will make sure we get what we deserve. . . . He could say whatever he wants and do lots of things, but this is something other people have to deal with, a cabinet and Congress, and if they don't pass anything, [Trump] won't be able to do much. Remember when the other one, Obama, was in office, he wanted to pass immigration reform, but they never let him. [Trump is] not going to be able to do what he wants just because he wants to. People get so scared, and that's why I'd rather not even watch the news at all a lot of the time. I'm busy making sure my food comes out good, my children are okay, that I'm okay, and I'm okay with everybody."

Aside from her confidence in herself, Mónica tells me she has faith in someone else: the sheriff of Santa Cruz County, where she lives. His name is Tony Estrada. Like Mónica, Tony was born in

Nogales, Sonora, Mexico. When he was a child, his family moved to the other Nogales, in Arizona, where Tony grew up and started his career in law enforcement as a dispatcher for the city's police department. He rose through the ranks until retiring as a captain, in 1991. Two years later, he was elected sheriff of Santa Cruz, a county that encompasses the cities of Nogales, Rio Rico, and Tubac, among others.

For twenty-four years, Tony has enjoyed the affection and support of the people. In an area known for drug trafficking, undocumented border crossers, and human trafficking, Tony has tried to stay in direct contact with local residents and understand their needs and the day-to-day reality of the community. In March 2017, Tony gained some new admirers not only in Arizona but across the country after an interview with *USA Today* was published in which he openly and directly expressed his disgust with Donald Trump's policies.[8]

"When he said Mexicans were rapists and drug traffickers, he insulted my people. The wall is a symbol; it sends a bad message, and it makes everything more dangerous, because when you push people out into the canyons and ravines, they're more vulnerable to the 'coyotes,' the traffickers," Tony told the newspaper, referring to migrants who cross undocumented. "It's a cruel way to control illegal immigration. When I was growing up, I lived on both sides of the border, from one to the other, because my family was one big community, and it was like that for a long time until they started to build the fence, that divided that relationship we've had for decades. What's come out of Washington is a fear that makes you feel like you might be questioned, even if you're a legal immigrant. People wonder, what's going to happen to my mom? To my brothers and sisters?"

In a letter dated January 31, 2017, Tony and twenty-eight other officials from the area, including the mayors of Brownsville and El Paso, Texas; judges; and congressional representatives signing as "members of the vibrant Mexico-U.S. border community," wrote to members of Congress asking them to oppose Trump's "reckless policies" on the border with Mexico, "our neighbor and trading partner." The letter closed with an invitation: "We encourage you to visit the Border communities that will be impacted by President Trump's tactics. We would welcome the opportunity for you to learn first-hand about our already safe and secure communities as well as the economic importance of the U.S.-Mexico border."[9]

CHAPTER SEVEN

LIFE IS NO DISNEYLAND

Yunuen Bonaparte, twenty-seven
Uruapan, Michoacán/Azusa, California

AUGUST 5, 2016, marked a turning point in Hillary Clinton's relationship with the press. Two hundred days into her presidential campaign, she had still not taken a single question from reporters. But on that day, the Democratic Party's nominee broke her silence and answered questions from Latino journalists, even discussing her email account under FBI investigation, the sore spot in her campaign.

"Now, I think journalists have a special responsibility to our democracy at a time like this," Clinton stated, her blond hair impeccably styled, wearing a turquoise suit and matching earrings as she addressed over fifteen hundred members of the National Association of Hispanic Journalists (NAHJ) and the National Association of Black Journalists (NABJ) in Washington, DC.[1]

While candidate Clinton fielded questions, Yunuen Bonaparte, a young NAHJ scholarship recipient and recent college graduate with a degree in communications, approached the podium. She raised her camera and took a photo of one of the most powerful women in the world.

Yunuen has lived more than half her life in Azusa, California. Originally from Uruapan, in Michoacán state, Mexico, she is a member of the "Dreamer" generation, young people who were brought to the United States undocumented by their parents when they were minors. They have grown up as Americans, with their lives and plans for the future rooted in this country, even though at this point they have no options open to them for legalizing their immigration status.

There are roughly two million young people in this situation in the US. The informal name for them, "Dreamers," comes from a legislative initiative first presented in Congress back in 2001 known as the DREAM (Development, Relief, and Education for Alien Minors) Act.[2] If passed, the law would allow undocumented people younger than thirty years of age who arrived in the US before they were sixteen and who have lived here for at least five years to gain temporary residency, with the possibility of applying for citizenship in the future. For nearly two decades, the DREAM Act has been presented in Congress on five occasions, failing to pass each time. Young people such Yunuen have begun their adult lives feeling part of a country that legally does not acknowledge them.

Yunuen does not have happy memories of her early childhood in Mexico. She remembers her family living in a poor neighborhood and never having a proper house. They lived in a shack cobbled together with scrap materials. She remembers her father working all kinds of jobs: at a stationery store, managing accounting for a company, selling curtains. She describes him as "a multiuse kind of person." But all of his hard work was still not enough to support the Bonaparte family. There was a time when they did not have any money to buy food and had to go to Yunuen's grandparents' house across the street to get something to eat.

When Yunuen's grandfather died, in 2001, the central figure in her family was gone. Her father decided to go to the US, while her mother stayed behind to take care of Yunuen, then eleven, her nine-year-old brother, and her one-year-old baby brother. Yunuen went to elementary school, and took care of her baby brother while her mother worked. The excellent grades she had always brought home in spite of the family's difficulties now began to drop. Around then, she failed a math test for the first time.

"I remember that was when my dad decided to send for us. The first thing I thought was that was good, because that way he wouldn't know I was failing math," she says without a trace of humor. "We had a small plot of land; my house was literally made out of cardboard. We lived in a big cardboard box, one bedroom, cots for me and my brother, the kitchen and bathroom combined. We didn't have a shower; we had to heat up water to take a bath. My parents sold the land and used the money to pay a coyote to bring us here."

Yunuen takes a sip of tea. She is petite but robust, with strong features, dark eyes with a sharp gaze, a smile that lights up her face, scrunching up her nose, making her look even younger and giving her a mischievous look. She wears her hair loose in a chin-length cut. We are at a coffee shop on Sunset Boulevard in Echo Park, Los Angeles. The neighborhood still bears traces of the Latino population that has largely been pushed out by the wave of gentrification affecting some areas of Southern California in recent years. Yunuen and I met through NAHJ, which we both belong to. Azusa, the small city where she lives, is forty minutes away from downtown Los Angeles.

She says that period of time is a bit fuzzy in her memory, and it's hard to remember the exact order of events. "I remember we went to Tijuana. It was my first time in an airplane, it was really weird. My uncle and aunt picked us up when we got there and took us to a hotel. I don't remember how long we were there, a few days or a week, I don't know."

The family spent those days or weeks at the hotel because the coyotes who were going to take them over to "the other side" were waiting for more people to show up. When enough people had arrived, around fifty, the coyote came and told them what time they would leave, and to be all packed and ready to go. From Tijuana, the group was taken to Los Algodones, a small town in the northwest corner of Baja California, right on the US border, where California and Arizona meet. There, they were installed in another hotel, shabbier than the first. Yunuen remembers it smelled like urine, with people packed in everywhere. She sat in a corner hoping that no one would look at her.

For the next leg of the journey, everyone was loaded into a pickup truck, "literally like sardines." Lying on top of each other, there were five layers of people. The three Bonaparte children were piled on last, and the truck started to move. Yunuen saw swirls of dust rising up from the dirt road as the truck bounced along. The men in the pickup's cabin yelled back at them to keep their heads down. When they came to a stop, they were packed into another motel, this time in the US.

Yunuen remembers sleeping with around twenty other people in a motel room there for one or two nights. Early in the morning, the group climbed into a refrigerated truck carrying lettuce. Shivering, they felt the truck start to move. Yunuen's baby brother, held in his mother's arms, started to cry. Yunuen tried to quiet him. Eventually the truck came to a stop. They heard voices outside, and then the door opened. It was immigration agents, "*la migra*." All of that for nothing.

After spending the night in a cell with fifty other people with only aluminum blankets protecting them from the cold, and only a cup of soup to eat, the next day they were shepherded down a corridor and passed through a gate. Yunuen's mother asked where they were. She was told they were in Tijuana.

Every year, approximately 175,000 people are detained and deported at the border, according to Immigration and Customs Enforcement data.[3] Although there are fifteen points of entry along the two-thousand-mile-long border, 25 percent of all deportations are into Tijuana. Over half of those detained at the border have crossed before at least once.

When Yunuen's mother found herself back at the starting point, she called the uncle who had picked them up before, and they started looking for another coyote. It was a woman this time. The family was taken to an apartment where some other families with children were already gathered, waiting. Everything seemed more secure, but it was also more expensive. The last coyote had charged $1,500 per person, but this one charged $3,000. Yunuen doesn't know how her family got the money. After just a few hours in the apartment, they started out, but this time was different. One by one, each member of the family crossed the border in a car. Yunuen was taken in a minivan. A woman drove, and another woman sat in the passenger seat. Yunuen lay down on the floor in the back-seat. As the minivan inched along in line approaching the border checkpoint, a vendor came by selling traditional woven blankets. The women bought a blanket and placed it over Yunuen. As they got closer, they told Yunuen not to move or make a sound, and to try to breathe very quietly. They pulled up to the booth, talked to the immigration agent inside for a minute, and then drove on through to the other side. And that was it.

Yunuen was the first in her family to cross. She was taken to a house in San Ysidro, a town right on the border, where some other families were already waiting. When her mother and brothers arrived, everyone was taken to Santa Ana, in Orange County, one hundred miles north of the border, between San Diego and Los Angeles. When Yunuen got out of the car, she saw that Disneyland was right across the street.

"Ever since then, I can't be anywhere near Disneyland," she says, not smiling. "I have never gone, because I was traumatized by all that. People get frustrated with me when I tell them I can't even drive by it."

Her uncle arrived, and finally the family reunited with her father.

"And we all lived happily ever after," Yunuen says with a sarcastic grin.

Starting a new life in the US is hard. Deciding to migrate may be the hardest decision many people ever have to make: leaving behind everything they know, their family and friends, their culture and support network. Starting over from nothing in a new place where they may not know anyone, may not speak the language, and do not understand the local ways represents a tremendous challenge. And if people are undocumented, their vulnerability to workplace exploitation, discrimination, and human rights violations is heightened considerably.

Yunuen's family chose to live in Azusa because one of her uncles already lived there. He had three children around the same ages as Yunuen and her siblings, which was helpful. For children, the hardest part of migrating is generally adapting to a new school system, in a new language, with a different academic structure and curriculum. Fortunately this was not too difficult for Yunuen, who had always been a strong student.

"I didn't speak English, but there were other kids in my school who didn't speak it either, so it wasn't such a big culture shock," Yunuen says. "I just had to try to pick it up. It took me two years to learn English. There were some other kids in my class who had been taking those classes for years, so that made me feel like I was doing pretty well. I was in seventh grade, and they were learning things I had already learned in fifth grade, so I didn't have to worry about things like math or geography, because I already knew it. I felt good, because I had been failing math before, but now I didn't have any problem, so I could really focus on learning English." By the time Yunuen entered high school she had a strong command of English. When she graduated, she had high marks in science and math, and one of the highest grade-point averages in her class.

Even though the adjustment at school was going well for Yunuen, her family's transition as a whole was more complicated. For families who arrive in the US with children, the period of adaptation is related to the children's integration into the school system and the understanding that they have a new home now. For Yunuen, the second issue is still unresolved, fifteen years later.

"When I got here, I never felt like I missed my home, because I've never known where my home was," she says. "I've always felt a little nostalgic for Mexico, but I know that if I went back, I wouldn't feel like it was my home. The problem is, I don't feel like here is my home either. But I think in my case that's because of some other things."

Those other things related to her family. When Yunuen was fifteen, three years after arriving in the US, her parents separated. As a result, Yunuen's mother had a nervous breakdown, which affected her ability to take care of her three children, but at the same time, she took out a restraining order against her children's father. The children were placed in foster care for three months.

"After that, I think we moved around about ten times in one year," says Yunuen. "The court decided my youngest brother should live with my mother, and my other brother, who's three years younger than me, and I went to live with my dad. The three of us were in one room, a garage." Yunuen's relationship with her mom has been strained ever since. "I think that's why I have this feeling of not knowing where my home is. I had to go into therapy for a while, but now it doesn't bother me so much. I live with my dad and that's fine, but it's not my home."

When Yunuen graduated high school, she took entrance exams for three colleges in the Los Angeles area. Her guidance counselor, who did not understand why Yunuen, such an excellent student, had not yet sent in any college applications, gave her fifty dollars for the application fees. Yunuen was accepted at all three schools, but she did not know how to explain that, even though she had been accepted, she could not go because she was undocumented and therefore ineligible for federal financial aid.

"I think people don't understand because they're not informed," she says. "This is happening; there are people all over the country in this situation. What they are going through should matter. But sometimes people just don't know about it."

In the United States, college costs $35,000 per year on average.[4] Those who cannot afford this—the great majority of students— can apply for financial aid provided by the government. But un- documented students cannot access this financial assistance, even though they have spent most of their lives growing up in the US. If they decide to go to college, they have to pay the same tuition as foreign students. For most undocumented students, the costs are too great, and getting a higher education is simply not an option. Many young people end up working in fast-food restaurants or at other jobs that do not require a college degree. Even those students who do manage to attend college and graduate have a hard time getting work because of their undocumented status.

After Yunuen graduated from high school, she had to get a job to start saving up money to attend community college, which costs much less than a traditional four-year college. For students who cannot afford four years of college tuition or simply do not want to go to school for four years, community colleges provide the option of getting a two-year degree at a much lower cost, or attending for two years and then transferring to a traditional college to earn a four-year degree. For students who want to go to college but have no access to financial aid, two years of community college at the sharply reduced cost provides some relief while they figure out how to earn a four-year degree.

Yunuen started working at a McDonald's when she was sixteen years old and still in high school. She continued working there after graduating, and added another part-time job at a photography studio. She enrolled in community college, taking classes when she could afford it, and worked at the photography studio for two more years after transferring to a four-year school. Later, when she was attending California State University at Fullerton (CSUF), she worked in a convenience store, first as a cashier, later stocking shelves in the early morning so she could take classes during the day.

Yunuen's circumstances changed along with those of hundreds of thousands of other Dreamers in 2012, when a small measure of relief came along for undocumented students bearing the crushing burden of working and going to college. In June of that year, President Barack Obama signed the Deferred Action for Childhood Arrivals (DACA) executive order, which temporarily protected Dreamers against deportation, giving them Social Security numbers and temporary work permits, as long as they met requirements similar to those in the DREAM Act.[5]

The temporary protection under this program would be in effect for two years, and could be renewed, as it was in 2014 and 2016. But since the program was not a law passed by Congress, it did not offer its beneficiaries legal residency or provide a pathway to citizenship. And just as Obama enacted it with a stroke of his pen, a future president could rescind it just as easily.

Even so, in the five years DACA has been in effect as of this writing, more than 750,000 young adults have seen a big change in their lives and have been able to realize their full potential.[6] Yunuen is one of the more than 200,000 DACA recipients in California.

Before the program, she looked for jobs wherever she could find them, doing whatever was needed but not necessarily what best suited her. She finished two years of community college in six years, paying all the costs out of her own pocket, and enrolled in CSUF in 2014.

Once at CSUF, Yunuen found a Dream Center, a resource for undocumented students that many colleges and universities now have. These centers were mostly created by Dreamers themselves, with the support of some faculty, and have been formalized at some schools, receiving funds for their administration. Students can find information there on financial aid and scholarships, as well as local legislative initiatives that could help them—since the DREAM Act has not passed Congress, many states like California have passed their own measures, giving undocumented students access to financial aid—and in recent years they can get assistance in applying for DACA. Most important of all, they discover a support network.

"I was shaking when I walked in. I didn't know what to do. It was really weird for me. Then these students there told me not to worry; they were there to help me. I told them I was studying communications and I wanted to work for a newspaper, and they told me the editor of the *Daily Titan*, the university newspaper, was interviewing people right then. That was so important to me! I was going to meet the editor of the paper!"

Many exciting things happened in the following months. Yunuen met other supportive faculty and students. By the end of the year, she was the president of the Latino student journalist group and had made connections with the National Association of Hispanic Journalists. Two years later, she found herself taking photos of Hillary Clinton for the organization at its national convention in Washington, DC.

"I think everything started happening when I said, 'I'm a Dreamer. This is what I do, and this is who I am,'" she says. "I've never been afraid to say it, but I think the fact that some other people understood what I was going through really helped me."

In May 2016, in her cap and gown, Yunuen graduated with a degree in communications. On her Facebook page, she posted a picture of her grades for her last semester, straight A's as usual, with the caption "That's a wrap." She wrote that her goals for the future were to find a job, stop watching episodes of *30 Rock* every day, and not get deported.

"Every day is a battle."

Yunuen stares off in the distance as she says this with a serious expression that makes her look older than her years. "I've gotten to a point where I'm happy with myself for what I've accomplished, but it's been really hard. My life plan was that I'd have a job by the time I was eighteen, and I'd move to my own place eventually, but that hasn't happened because I can't. I can't move out of my dad's place, because I can't afford to pay my own rent. Luckily, my dad has supported me, but I've always had this little voice inside of me saying 'You can't do that.' One of your friends is going to get a master's degree? You can't do that. When I told my family I wanted to be a photographer, it was really hard to talk to my dad about it, to tell him, 'I want to get an education and not work in a factory being miserable for the rest of my life.' My dad would say, 'Why do you have to go to school to learn how to take pictures? Go to school so you can make money.' I explained I didn't want to be frustrated doing something else, and his answer was, 'Who told you that you can do what you want in life?' I was still in school, and he asked me to help out with the rent. He's always taken care of us, but we've always had money problems. And I realized, you go to school and all your friends say my mom tells me I can do whatever I want in life. But for me, it's always been different."

At this point in her story, Yunuen can't hold back the tears now streaming down her face, as if a faucet had been turned on. A waiter comes by and discreetly clears away her empty mug of tea. Yunuen sobs a little, then pauses for a while. When she feels ready to continue, she tells me there were times at community college when she was hungry but only had a dollar in her bank account. She tells me the hardest part about being undocumented goes beyond simply not having papers; the hardest part is the impossibility of earning money to do what you really want to do. You have to get accustomed to that idea and learn to live with it. If you stopped to think about all of the horrible things that could happen to you on any given day, you couldn't go on living. She tells me that before she had a driver's license—she has a temporary one now because of DACA—she could not let herself think about what might happen if she was pulled over: the cost of the fine; the cost of getting the car back if it was impounded, which was more than a thousand dollars at the time; the things that you can't avoid when you're undocumented. She tells me that once she had to go to court to explain to a judge why she had been driving without a license. The judge asked Yunuen why she didn't have a license and she said, "Because I can't get one." The judge asked why not. She said, "Because I'm undocumented." He let her go.

"You put it at the back of your mind and keep going, but that's the hardest part. No one else has to live that way, worried they might get stopped by the police. No one else has to worry that their little brother won't have a way to get to school, not because you don't know how to drive, but because you're not allowed."

In October 2016, the Center for American Progress, a progressive think tank, published a study evaluating DACA four years after it went into effect, which was prompted by Donald Trump's campaign promises to rescind DACA as soon as he was sworn into office if he won the presidential election.[7] Of the program's 750,000 beneficiaries, of whom 77 percent are Mexican, 95 percent are currently either attending school or working, or both. Of those working, 63 percent say they have gotten a better job, 49 percent switched to a job that was a better fit for their education level and degree, and their average salary rose by 42 percent, meaning the amount they paid in taxes increased too. Of all the DACA recipients, 6 percent have launched their own businesses, compared with 3.1 percent on average nationally. Many of these entrepreneurs are creating jobs, including one who has nine employees. Overall, these young people have had to constantly face and overcome daunting challenges, and as a result have become successful—some might even say invincible.

I share this information with Yunuen as we talk at the cafeteria on Sunset Boulevard, and tell her that after hearing her story, I have this image of her: a twenty-seven-year-old woman, photojournalist, bilingual, coming from difficult financial circumstances, who has worked to support herself and pay for her education, first at community college, then at a university. After graduation, she has worked as a volunteer and has had her work published in several media outlets—in December 2016, her photos were included in an article on migrant women field workers that was published on the cover of *El Universal,* one of the biggest newspapers in Mexico. Against all the odds, Yunuen is successful.

"It doesn't feel like that, though," she responds. "I think if I didn't have to go through all this, things would have been different. I don't know if I'd be where I am now, but . . ."—she starts to cry again—"I think I would have been able to accomplish more. I think I would have my own place to live by now, the way I want to live. Now I always feel like it will never be enough. I focus on doing things I want to do, but there are always limits, and there's nothing I can do about it. Even when I've come so far, it feels like everything just happened by chance, and something's always telling me I don't deserve it."

When I ask her why she thinks that is, she shares an anecdote. She recently reconnected on social media with Anita, an old friend from grade school back in Michoacán. Anita's mother has cancer, and Anita works in a Walmart to help support the family. "I have no idea how they got a Walmart there," Yunuen comments, surprised. Anita's younger sister is married to a drug addict, with three children. Yunuen can't help but think her life would have turned out similarly if her family had not migrated.

"I think that would have been my life," she says with a guilty look. "I'm so lucky to be here, to be able to do everything I do. But still I want more. I don't want to have fight against all these obstacles all the time, because every day I have to think, Where am I going to be a few months from now? Will I have a job?"

Every time the issue of undocumented immigration comes up for national debate, with all the limitations it represents for undocumented people in the US, an obligatory question is raised that almost every undocumented immigrant has had to answer: Wouldn't it be easier if you just went back to your country? Yunuen laughs when I say this, because it's a question she has indeed answered many times before.

"We're here for a reason," she says. "When my family and I got ready to come here, we literally didn't have anything to eat at home for a few months before we left. My mom planted vegetables out behind the house, but she didn't have any money to buy tortillas. It was hard to survive. I don't know what would have happened to us if we hadn't come here, but we weren't in that situation because my dad was lazy; it was because there was no work. I don't think of myself as a brilliant person, but I've always done well in school, and at that time I was having trouble because I was distracted. I know that I probably wouldn't have been able to go to school, definitely not to college. I know in Mexico there are free public colleges, but that's not the problem. The problem is you have to survive financially to be able to go to school."

Even though Yunuen is well aware of what her future would look like in her city of origin—her cousins who still live there have a difficult time finding work, and violence in the state has risen sharply as a result of the war on narco-trafficking—it's a possibility she has been forced to consider. On September 5, 2017, Donald Trump announced that he would not renew the DACA program and would begin phasing it out within six months.[8] If Congress fails to pass legislation protecting the Dreamers, young people like Yunuen will be vulnerable to deportation once again. And a deportation could happen at any time.

"I have talked about it with some of my friends, and they always say, 'I have family there; you can always stay with them if that happens.' Okay, even though I have a college degree, I don't think it means anything. I don't know if I could work as a journalist there—they kill so many journalists! I know with my network of friends I could find something, like a receptionist job or something like that. I haven't been there in so many years, and things have changed. When I was little, I remember one day the newspaper published a story about finding a dead body a block away from my school in front of a butcher shop; that was in 2002. I remember the picture of the butcher shop and the body, and all the blood. It was a big story. Now that happens all the time; they find a body every day. I still have family there, and things have happened to them. They live their lives just hoping nothing else happens."

Then, with an inner strength that has allowed her to keep moving ahead every time it seems like there is no way forward, Yunuen tells me in a rush that while she understands what this country has given her, she's also aware of what she has to give back.

"As a photojournalist, how can you tell stories about minority women if you're a white man? I know some people can be empathetic when they hear these stories, but if they don't understand the experience, if you don't understand where they're coming from, you'll never get the whole story," she says. "I see that the newspapers appreciate the sensibility that people like me can bring to the work, that no one else can. I'm sure there are other documented journalists who can do the same thing as me, and I still have a lot to learn in my work, but I think that because of my experience, I have the right perspective to tell this story like no one else, through my eyes. How do you tell a Guatemalan child's story? Are you going to ask him, 'Tell me how it feels to be in a cell in immigration'? I've been in an immigration cell, I can tell you. I can tell you about the names on the walls, for example—a lot of people write their names in the cell and how many times they've crossed the border, and leave messages of hope. I remember the message of a woman who said, 'I've tried twenty times and I'll keep trying.'" Yunuen quotes this in Spanish. "And I thought, How many times am I going to have to try? There were double-digit numbers in there. No one should have to try something in the double digits to have a better life, and people don't do it because the United States is so wonderful, or because they want to get rich. It's because they need to provide for their families because they have no other way to survive. So I think I can tell this story a little better. If we don't tell their stories from that perspective, they will keep on being just numbers instead of people."

Yunuen knows that DACA has been, as she puts it, "a Band-Aid." Although she has always been careful, she has felt much freer with DACA. Now she knows that under the Trump administration, the risks will be much greater, but she refuses to hide.

"I'm not going to hide anymore," she says. "My dad has the attitude, 'Don't tell anybody; don't tell the neighbors you're undocumented.' I'm just being more careful. Now it's not so much about what will happen back there if they deport me but the fact that they would take away the place where I belong. Even though I still don't feel like this is my home, I feel like I do contribute to society in some way. I don't have a criminal record and don't wish anyone harm. I'm just a person trying to live. Why can't I have the chance to make a living?"

Yunuen's latest photography project is a series of portraits of DACA recipients, like her, along with the answers they gave when asked what they would do if they lost the program's protection. But she has not been very public about her immigration status before, until this year. On January 27, a few hours after President Trump signed an executive order banning people from certain countries from entering the US, known as the Muslim ban, Yunuen posted on her Facebook page: "Here's my revolutionary act for the day: I'm #UndocumentedAndUnafraid and I'm #HereToStay."

CHAPTER EIGHT

CAPTAIN OF HIS PEOPLE

Al Labrada, forty-seven

Mexico City/Los Angeles, California

ON MARCH 22, 2017, the Los Angeles Police Department announced a slate of officer promotions. Among them was Alfred "Al" Labrada, who was promoted from lieutenant to captain. Al's journey to that culminating moment had begun back in 1975, when he crossed the border from Mexico, undocumented, along with his mother and siblings. At that time, the thought of an undocumented Mexican boy living in East Los Angeles growing up to become a high-ranking police officer would have sounded like a wild pipe dream. Four decades later, Al was responsible for community relations at the LAPD, the third-largest police department in the country.

Now, at a time when the president of the United States hurls denigrating accusations against Mexican immigrants, hundreds of kids whose families, some undocumented, came to this country in search of better opportunities see themselves reflected in Captain Labrada's story. They know that today, that opportunity is real.

When Al was just two years old, his father died. His mother had to raise the children on her own, and after three years she had saved up enough money to migrate to the United States. Al was only five years old when they crossed the border and doesn't remember it clearly, but he knows they arrived first in Rosemead, California, undocumented, and later moved to El Monte.

Like many migrant women when they first arrive in the US, Al's mother got to work cleaning houses. There is a large population of immigrants, mostly Latino, in southeast Los Angeles County today, but Al remembers there were not so many back then. His mother mainly worked for white families in the city of Arcadia. Some were nice, while others were downright rude and disrespectful. Al recalls a general atmosphere of intimidation.

"I remember being really afraid of traveling. We had family in San Diego and other parts of California, and we would take the Greyhound bus, because we didn't have a car for a long time, and we were really scared to go through the checkpoint in San Clemente, where they sometimes check your papers. That's what I remember from that time, when I was a kid, always being a little afraid," Al recalls. Even though his family gained legal status when he was thirteen, that feeling of uncertainty stayed with him for some time after.

When he was sixteen, Al began working at a Taco Bell restaurant to help out his mother and three siblings. He also started thinking about joining the military. He liked the discipline he saw in members of the armed forces, the opportunity that enlisting would give him to go to college at a time when his family did not have much money, and that it would help him become a citizen. His mother did not like the idea of the military much, but she did want her son to have the chance to get a higher education, so Al enlisted in the Army Reserves, which accelerated his naturalization process. At eighteen, Al became a US citizen. He started college and then was called up to go to Iraq, where he spent a year fighting in the Gulf War.

Al's decision to join the military is not unusual within the Latino community in the United States, especially in states with a large concentration of Latinos, such as California and Texas. In 2015, 12 percent of the active service members in the armed forces were Hispanic, three times more than in 1980.[1] Many enlist because they identify with the sense of discipline Al describes, but also because it facilitates access to higher education, which they would not otherwise have. In the US, two-thirds of Hispanics who start working or enlist in the armed forces right out of high school instead of going on to college say they made that decision based on the necessity of helping out their family financially. In contrast, only a third of white young adults cite their family's financial circumstances as a reason for not going to college.[2]

In 2013, I had the chance to attend the Memorial Day ceremony held at the National Cemetery in Riverside, California. It is the third-largest military cemetery in the country, and it has received the most fallen soldiers of any since 2000. No matter how many similar scenes one has seen before, in magazines or movies, or how many stories one has read about it, it's impossible not to be deeply moved, watching families remember their loved ones who died in combat: the twenty-two-year-old man who did not come back from Iraq, his impossibly young widow cradling his photo in her arms, or the Vietnam War veteran there to pay his respects to another soldier killed in that war.

Memorial Day always evokes mixed emotions. On the one hand, some people believe the deaths are the price we pay for the freedoms we enjoy in this country; on the other hand, some believe wars are fought over economic or corporate interests or misguided national politics, and that enlisted soldiers are seen as disposable tools used to accomplish the government's goals.

Among all the faces etched with pain I saw that day, I was struck by how many Latinos were there. Some wore the insignias of their military units, or symbols representing the veterans groups they joined after returning home, or the places they had been deployed. The words "Vietnam," "Iraq," and "Afghanistan" could be seen over and over again embroidered on shirts and jackets worn by young men with last names like Rodríguez and Gutiérrez.

Twelve percent of the active armed forces in the country represents more than 150,000 people. Some branches are more popular than others: the Navy is 14 percent Latino, while the Marines are 15 percent. The number of Latinos in the military is large partly because it can be a path to citizenship for some undocumented immigrants. Also, the military conducts aggressive recruitment campaigns in Latino neighborhoods under the slogan, in Spanish,

"*Yo soy el Army*"—"I am the Army." The recruitment officers are also usually Latino, and they go directly inside schools with large Latino student populations and even visit people's homes, tactics not generally practiced in the case of other ethnic groups. In this campaign, recruiters emphasize access to higher education through joining the military. In a poll conducted in 2012, 12 percent of Latinos who enlisted said the chance to go to college was their primary reason for signing up.[3]

Looking back, it may be hard for Al and others his age to identify their strongest motivation for enlisting in the military several decades ago. One thing is certain: the experience changed their lives. In Al's case, he returned home in 1992 determined to continue his education and to become a fireman or policeman. In the end, he opted for the latter.

On September 5, 2010, a Los Angeles police officer fired on Manuel Jamines in front of MacArthur Park. According to police reports, the officer feared for his safety after ordering Jamines, who was allegedly carrying a knife, to stop and put his hands in the air. The officer gave the order several times, in Spanish and in English. An immigrant from Guatemala, Jamines did not understand either; he only spoke Quiché, an indigenous language. He was shot in the head and torso and died at the scene.

This case sparked protests and charges of police abuse from local Latino activists, some asserting that Jamines had not been carrying a knife. But it also shined a spotlight on an issue that has worried indigenous migrant organizations for years in California: while trying to help immigrants who do not speak English integrate into US society, the authorities and public servants who are partly responsible for their integration must be informed and educated so that the end result is a success, or at least to make sure the integration effort does not end in senseless tragedy.

Although California is among the states that have made the most progress in terms of recognizing the rights of people who speak a language other than English, offering translation and interpreting services in different languages in government offices and social service agencies, a common mistake is to assume that all immigrants from Latin America speak Spanish as a first language. In courts, hospitals, and police stations, a Spanish interpreter is assigned to someone who needs to make a statement, even if that person's knowledge of Spanish is minimal or nonexistent. The consequences of this error range from legal complications to inadequate health care, and even death.

The issue of racism occupies an important place in US history, but it is usually discussed in terms of a black/white, African American/Anglo-Saxon dichotomy. The reality is much more complicated, involving Native Americans, Asians, and, of course, Latinos. And that is rarely discussed. There does not seem to be any cohesive registry or timeline that explains, or at least defines, the violence committed by the state against Latinos.

According to data from the US Department of Justice's Office of Justice Programs, even though Hispanics make up only 17 percent of the population, they represent 23 percent of people detained by police to be searched and 30 percent of arrests.[4] Among minority groups, Latinos account for the second-highest number of killings at the hands of police, after African Americans: 16 percent and 25 percent overall, respectively.[5]

This is nothing new. Al Labrada remembers being stopped by police as a youth in El Monte. When he would go to visit relatives in the Highland Park neighborhood of Los Angeles, he saw how the police treated Latinos, and he did not like it at all. He noticed that sometimes police would stop people for no apparent reason, and they were very disrespectful. There were no Latino police officers and very few female officers. Al thought if there were more Latino officers who could identify with the people in the community, maybe things would get better. So one day he went to the police station and asked how he could join. In May 1993, he entered the police academy.

"Back then, Latinos were just starting to join the LAPD. Where I was, there were forty officers and only five of us were Latinos. Now, we're 48 percent Latino, and I've seen academy classes with

60 percent," he says with obvious pride, describing Hispanic representation among the ten thousand officers in the LAPD.

Hispanics are the fastest-growing ethnic group in police departments across the country.[6] In 2013, they represented 12 percent of officers working full-time, a 7 percent increase over their numbers in the 1980s. In spite of this growth, they are still underrepresented, with Hispanics currently making up 17 percent of the US population.

A survey conducted in 2016[7] found that Hispanic police officers have conflicted feelings about their work. Two-thirds said that their jobs often or almost always made them feel proud, and half said they felt satisfied or fulfilled. Still, many expressed discontent: half said their jobs almost always made them feel frustrated, and one out of five said their work often made them feel angry.

Seven of every ten thought incidents of police violence against African Americans have made their jobs more difficult, and now officers in their departments are less likely to stop and question people when they see something suspicious. Six of every ten Hispanic and African American officers said identifying undocumented immigrations should be the federal government's responsibility, in contrast with the 60 percent of white officers who believe the police should play a more active role.

"A lot of people don't know where police officers come from, their personal stories, that could be interesting and could help people identify with them," says Al. He is the perfect example of this: in 2000, he was promoted to sergeant; in 2014, he became a lieutenant; in 2017, he achieved the rank of captain. The man who as a teen dreamed of changing how the police treat immigrants has been in the ranks of the LAPD himself for almost a quarter century.

"There are officers from Oaxaca, El Salvador, or Guatemala who came to the US with a lot of hardship," he says. "People don't know the officers experienced the same problems as many of them: they've been undocumented, or their parents are undocumented; they've confronted racism and abuse; they have themselves experienced many of the situations that we're talking about across the whole country right now."

The first time I saw Al Labrada, a lieutenant with the LAPD at the time, was at a community meeting in the Koreatown neighborhood of downtown Los Angeles. Fourteen police officers dressed in full uniform, complete with guns on their belts, arrived punctually at the meeting space that is also where CBDIO, the Centro Binacional para el Desarrollo Indígena Oaxaqueño, holds its events. In cooperation with the Indigenous Front of Binational Organizations (FIOB), the LAPD was holding its eighth annual Cultural Awareness Workshop for public servants and staff of nongovernmental organizations. The workshop aimed to educate those responsible for providing services in immigrant communities and law enforcement on the ethnic diversity, culture, and customs of indigenous communities.

"Overall, we got a positive response from police officers," observed Gaspar Rivera-Salgado, project director at UCLA's Center for Labor Research and Education and a founder of FIOB. "The challenge sometimes can be Latino officers who get annoyed because they're going to get another lecture on migrant communities from their countries of origin. They think they know it all already. But that changes when they find out that, no, they don't know everything."

At the beginning of the workshop, the apathy of some officers was clear, but that gradually changed as the presentations continued. Rivera-Salgado talked about the special challenges of learning English, or any other foreign language, for those who speak an indigenous language and do not know how to read or write. Learning another language is an educational process, and you need to have the infrastructure in place for that. If you are illiterate in your own language, it is unlikely you will be able to become proficient in another language.

Another issue is linguistic diversity among people who come from apparently similar regions. The workshop presenters patiently displayed maps of southern Mexico, pointing out the differences among linguistic families. Although Zapotec is spoken in several regions, variations of the language could mean that people from different areas would not understand each other even if they come from the same Mexican state. For example, they explained that people from Oaxaca not only may speak more than one Zapotec dialect, they may also speak Mixtec, Chatino, or Triqui. How, then, do you communicate with someone when they have been identified simply as speaking an "indigenous language"? By now the officers attending the workshop are paying close attention, waiting to hear the answer. A Mexican man in the audience helped a fellow activist who was African American to understand these differences. He used the word "tortilla" as an example, which has one meaning in Mexico, a staple food made from flour or corn, while in Spain it means a dish made of eggs, potatoes, and onions. Mexico and Spain are both Spanish-speaking countries. "So is it a different language?" the second man asked. "No, it's the same language, but that word doesn't mean the same thing." A white officer listened closely and took notes. Al smiled with satisfaction.

"The police department works to ensure a lack of communication does not become a factor in cases like the Jamines case, and to build trust among the immigrant community in general, especially the indigenous community and law enforcement," Al told me after the workshop. "We know there are people who don't report domestic violence or call emergencies in to 911 because they have no way to communicate."

Three years after that workshop, I talked with Al over the phone. It was early 2017. Donald Trump had just been sworn into office, and the mayor of Los Angeles, Eric Garcetti, had renewed his commitment to the city to maintain Los Angeles's status as a sanctuary city. Local authorities, specifically the LAPD, would not perform any immigration enforcement, because that is the federal government's responsibility. I mentioned the Cultural Awareness Workshop to Al and asked if LAPD leadership still took the same approach.

"At first, a lot of officers didn't really understand why that was part of their job, why it was important," he explained. "A lot of the younger officers want to go out on the streets and go after bad guys, the ones committing crimes, to get guns off the streets, but they don't think about building trust in the community. We still believe the only way to get the 'bad guys' is to understand how each community works and what is causing fear and distrust. We're still doing our job."

It's Friday night, and a sign outside a house in southern Los Angeles announces it's *"viernes* [Friday] *de tlayudas."* With the catchy slogan *"Tlayúdate que yo tlayudaré,"* riffing off the Spanish phrase *"Ayúdate que yo te ayudaré,"* or "God helps those who help themselves," Oaxacan members of the Indigenous Front of Binational Organizations prepare their traditional dish, *tlayudas*, to sell in the community, and at the same time hold informational seminars to prepare for possible attacks on the immigrant community under the Trump administration.

"The first thing I want to reiterate is that the Los Angeles police are not going to detain immigrants just for being undocumented," says Al.

Al Labrada would be promoted to captain just a few days later, but his work in community relations, especially among Latino immigrants, had already been known for years among activists and residents of neighborhoods in the city's center, south, and southeast. Tall, good-looking, with dark hair and eyes and a friendly smile, Al gives his talks in Spanish, in a professional manner, while still speaking colloquially, coming across as approachable and down-to-earth.

"We've said it before: we have more than enough work dealing with local criminals," he says. "We're not going to start doing immigration agents' jobs too."

Al has a freshly made *tlayuda* waiting for him on the table, but before digging in, he talks to the audience of thirty or so people who have come to ask questions: What's going to happen if I report a case of domestic violence and they ask for my documents? What should I do if an immigration agent comes to my house? If people have a prior arrest—Trump had said he would deport criminals— how can they protect themselves? If the kids are Dreamers with DACA, will they get arrested first?

Al answers every question in a reassuring tone. Keep in mind that although Trump can sign executive orders, he explains, no new budget has been approved to hire more immigration agents, so the number of arrests will not go up for now.

If someone is detained, he or she has the right to go before a judge, but there is no budget to hire enough judges either, so it can take years for the court dates to come around. Al notes that some people who have been detained recently have court dates in 2019, then a few years in the future. Since there is no new money for detention centers, either, it would be impossible to keep everyone locked up in detention until then, as people are released under their own recognizance until their court dates. And in the meantime, there will have been new elections for Congress, and the next presidential election will be right around the corner. But that doesn't mean people should let their guard down.

When Al finishes talking and finally sits down to eat his now-cold *tlayuda*, Roberto Foss, an immigration lawyer, takes over. A self-described "gringo," Foss speaks Spanish well, using a couple of swear words that gain his listeners' trust. He explains that an executive order such as those Trump signed in his first two weeks in office do not change immigration laws currently in effect; only Congress can do that. The one thing that could change is the status of DACA recipients. And even then, Foss says he doubts there would suddenly be massive arrests of those young people. He stresses that people need to be informed, know their rights, and try not to succumb to fear.

"I'm not going to tell you not to worry, but I will tell you to be informed. I don't think here in Los Angeles somebody's going to show up at your front door, but you do need to know how the system works so you know what to do: ask for a lawyer, stay silent, do not sign anything, and fight your case to the end. The courts are still there to decide," Foss says to the attendees who have come for something more than a delicious *tlayuda*.

That very night, as Foss was discussing legal resources, a judge in Washington State ruled against Trump's executive order known as the Muslim ban and ordered its temporary suspension on a national level. The next day, Trump lost again when an appeals court refused to reinstate the travel ban.[8]

A few days later, Al told me that what the LAPD was most worried about was the growing fear of immigration raids among undocumented people. Since Trump's election, unfounded rumors had spread widely on social media about ICE agents arresting people on the streets. People get scared, and their distrust grows along with their fear.

"Sometimes we have no control over the things causing fear," Al said. "It's often just wrong information; then you have to work with those communities. A lot of people don't know what goes on in the streets with violence, the situations police have to deal with. There are 1.2 million contacts with LAPD officers and the public every year, and less than 0.5 percent result in violence. But there is distrust; that's a fact. We have to work in the communities across the whole country to gain their trust, because these incidents cause anxiety, not just in the community but in us, too, because we don't know how the community is going to react."

Al has an eleven-year-old son who says he wants to be an astronaut when he grows up. It might seem far-fetched for the child of a Mexican who came to the US undocumented to dream of being an astronaut, but in the Labrada family, opportunities are well earned.

CHAPTER NINE

FAMILIES CAUGHT BETWEEN TWO WORLDS

Guadalupe García de Rayos, thirty-five
Acámbaro, Guanajuato/Phoenix, Arizona

Noemí Romero, twenty-five
Villahermosa, Tabasco/Glendale, Arizona

Viridiana Hernández, twenty-six
Jojutla, Morelos/Phoenix, Arizona

ON FEBRUARY 8, 2017, Guadalupe García de Rayos showed up for a check-in appointment with immigration authorities in Phoenix, Arizona, just as she had every six months for the last eight years. Nine years earlier, in 2008, Lupita was detained in one of Maricopa County sheriff Joe Arpaio's raids for using a false Social Security number. Her lawyer appealed, and she was released on the condition that she regularly appear for check-ins while her case was resolved.

The day after her detention, on February 9, Lupita, thirty-five and the mother of two US-citizen children, was deported to Nogales, Sonora. Her children and her husband, also undocumented, stayed in Arizona. Lupita's case received wide media coverage, since she had the dubious distinction of being the first Mexican to be deported by the Trump administration.

Throughout his presidential campaign, Trump said that if elected, he would prioritize deporting criminals. But under the executive orders he signed five days after taking office, modifying immigration guidelines, almost any undocumented person who had ever used false documents to get a job would have been categorized as having committed a crime, whether or not they had a criminal record. By this criterion, people like Lupita became targets for deportation.

Although no large-scale deportations took place in the following months—which of course does not guarantee that they will not happen in the future—Lupita's case illustrated one of the biggest and least discussed problems in the immigration debate: there are nine million people living in the United States with mixed-status families. Of those, four million are undocumented parents, and a half million are children who lack documentation, even though they grew up here. The remaining four and a half million are citizen children who enjoy the benefits that come with being born in the US every day.[1] What happens in a family when the parents are undocumented while the children aren't, or when children in the same family have a different immigration status? What is it like for families when one member has access to all the services and privileges that come with citizenship, but another does not?

I first met the Romero family in 2013 on a trip to Arizona. In this household, the three children were taught that everyone was equal. They were raised to respect their elders, to be proud of their country of origin, and to love the United States, where they had lived for twenty years. But deep down, they all knew they were not the same: though Cynthia, the youngest, was a US citizen, her older siblings, Steve and Noemí, were undocumented.

In recent years, the number of children born in the US to undocumented parents has risen, and as a result more families are living with the tension that comes when members of mixed status are living under the same roof. Though older children may lack documents because they were brought to this country when they were small, the youngest children tend to be citizens. According to the most recent data available, as of 2013 there were more than five million children in the US with at least one undocumented parent. Eight out of ten of those children, a little more than four million, are US citizens.[2]

Of the three Romero children, Noemí, then twenty-one years old, was the first to understand what their different status meant. When she was fifteen and her friends from school started taking the test to get a driver's license, Noemí asked her parents why she couldn't get one. María, her mother, explained the situation and why Noemí would be denied access to other privileges in the years to come.

Noemí found out what some of those other privileges were when she decided she wanted to continue her education after high school. She found that colleges opened their doors to her only to slam them shut when she let them know she did not have a Social Security number. Then she realized that of the three children in her family, getting a higher education would be a privilege reserved only for Cynthia, who was thirteen years old at the time.

"There's so much tension you feel," María Gómez, the mother of the Romero children, told me. Like her husband, María was undocumented. We met in Phoenix at an event organized by Puente, one of the most visible pro-immigrant activist groups in Arizona. Originally from the Mexican state of Tabasco, in 1995 the couple and their two small children, three-year-old Noemí and one-year-old Steve, came to live in Glendale, Arizona. Cynthia was born five years later.

"As they got older, they figured it out," María said of her two oldest kids. "I told them we couldn't go to Mexico for a few reasons. Well, okay, we could go, but how would we get back? They didn't understand it very well at first, but they accepted it."

The Romero children went to school and grew up as Americans, like everyone else. But once they entered adulthood, the difference between being documented and being undocumented took a toll on the family's stability: compounding the frustration generated by opportunities denied to her siblings, Cynthia lived with the fear that someone in her family, including her parents, could be deported at any moment.

Children in families where one or both parents are undocumented grow up with certain disadvantages. Much has been written about how the children of undocumented parents tend to score lower on cognitive development and achievement tests in school compared to their peers because their family incomes tend to be low. Families have fewer resources to devote to their children's activities and supervision, and they have less autonomy because they depend on whatever jobs they can get, which are not necessarily those they are best qualified for. Children of undocumented immigrants tend to have fewer years of formal education than children of documented immigrants.

Ever since she was little, Cynthia, the youngest Romero child, had to serve as a bridge between her family and the outside world. As is common in Latino communities, Cynthia's primary language is English, but she understands Spanish perfectly well since her parents speak it at home. This means she plays an important role in her family's communications. As we were talking, even though I asked her every question in English, Cynthia answered me in Spanish, out of courtesy to her mother, who was with us.

"I help my mother, for example, when she goes to make a deposit at the bank or when we go to see her lawyer, who doesn't speak Spanish," Cynthia said. "I want to be a lawyer too, to help out our . . ." She paused, searching for the right word in Spanish. "To help our community."

Although Cynthia still had several years before she would need to decide on a career path, at that moment her choice of future profession was certainly influenced by what her family had experienced in recent years. In 2010, María was arrested and taken to an immigration detention center in Arizona, where she was held for four weeks.

Deportation proceedings were opened, and María's case had still not been resolved in court. Her lawyer had told her clearly from the beginning that the deportation process takes years to be completed and informed her that a delay wins time so parents can be with their children and the family can be together in the United

States. But if María's final court date was not postponed by 2015, María would be deported.

According to Immigration and Customs Enforcement (ICE) data, in 2013 one of every six people deported, more than seventy thousand people, said they had one or more children who had been born in the US.[3] Their deportations not only separated families but deprived one or more US citizens of the right to live in their country with their parents.

"Since then, and even today, Cynthia thinks about what will happen when that moment comes, because she really doesn't want to go to Mexico," María tells me, worried. "The weeks when I wasn't here were very hard for her. I told her to think positive, that something good was going to come of this, so she wasn't overwhelmed, because it is really stressful. But then with what happened to Noemí, that made everything worse."

Noemí had lived in the US for seventeen of her twenty years when, on June 15, 2012, President Obama announced the implementation of the Deferred Action for Childhood Arrivals (DACA) program. This was wonderful news for Noemí, who met all the requirements to apply. The only problem was the application fee, $465, which she did not have. She did not have a work permit either.

She decided to get a job to save up the money for the application. She starting working as a cashier at a convenience store, using a false name, earning $7.65 an hour. She had only been working there for a few weeks when an immigration raid put her behind bars at the Eloy Detention Center, under threat of deportation.

"It was awful. I wondered how they were doing at home, if the only one working was my father, to support the whole family, pay the rent, the bills, and on top of that, the lawyers to get me out," Noemí said. "I thought about my brother, that someday they're going to get him too. Or my dad, he's undocumented too. And I thought about Cynthia, what's going to happen to her if they send us all back to Mexico?"

María was desperate. Noemí was locked up in detention for four months while the family tried to find lawyers to help. Cynthia translated from English into Spanish so her parents understood. The family also grappled with the uncertainty of what to do if Noemí was deported. Could they leave her on her own in Mexico, where she did not know anyone?

Thanks to help from Puente, Noemí was released. But in a bitter irony, her situation worsened: since she had pleaded guilty to using a false name to get a job and save up money to apply for DACA, she now had a criminal record, making her ineligible for the program. "Now, there's nothing for me," she said with a look of profound sadness.

Facing the dismal prospects of her own case, Noemí is concerned that an eventual move by her family to Mexico would shut down Cynthia's chance at the education she and her brother could never have because of their undocumented status. "It's not fair that Cynthia, who was born here with all the rights of a citizen, would have to go with us just because we can't be here legally. Sometimes I do feel bad that I don't have those privileges, and that there are people here who have them but just don't take advantage of them. I just want my sister . . ."—Noemí pauses and starts to cry, overcome with emotion—"to appreciate what she has, what my brother and I couldn't do. I want her to do it for us."

A few minutes later, after Cynthia has left the room, María expressed her worries a bit more openly. "At home we talk about it very clearly, because my process ends in 2015. Then we had Noemí's situation, and my husband could be detained at any time, like any of us, and what do we do? I can't be separated from any of my three children, either we all go, or we all stay. Cynthia gets upset and says, 'Why me, Mom?' She says she is not going, and that's it. But then, what do we do? That's a battle we have at home right now. I've thought about how we're going to need to get Cynthia some psychological help. I tell her not to think about it so much, because sometimes she'll say all day, 'Listen, I'm not going. What am I going to do over there?' talking about Mexico. I know it's not fair not only for her but my other two children, who are practically from here too. Sometimes the sense of guilt their father and I have, especially when Noemí was in prison . . . It's very hard to realize my daughter was locked up because I brought her here. I didn't consider the consequences of coming to a place that didn't want us."

After seeing what happened to her sister, Cynthia decided she wants to be a lawyer, like all the lawyers she had to talk to who helped get her sister out of prison. When I ask her what it feels like to be the only documented person in her family, she says, "Having papers is a privilege."

Two years after our conversation, in the summer of 2015, I tried to track down the Romero family to find out what had happened to them. I called the only contact number I had for them, María's cell phone. No one ever answered.[4]

Of all the young pro-immigrant activists I have met, Viridiana Hernández is one of those with the strongest presence. With a light-brown complexion, black hair, and dark-brown eyes contrasting with her bright smile, for most of her life Viri, as her friends call her, has lived the contradiction of being in a mixed-status family.

Originally from Jojutla, in Morelos state, Viri was brought to live in Arizona when her mother decided to risk it all for the chance to give her baby daughter a better life. Her parents, Viri's grandparents, were already living in the US legally, because they had worked in the Bracero Program for several years. Viri's mom could not get legal status herself, because of age limits established in US law for the children of braceros, so she crossed the border undocumented, and arrived in Phoenix with her little girl in her arms.

Like so many others of the Dreamer generation, Viridiana has no idea what her birthplace is like. Sometimes her grandparents show her photos they have taken on visits back to Morelos, and ask her if she remembers a particular place or relative in the pictures. Viri only laughs and says, "How could I remember, if I was only one year old?"

"I always knew I was from Mexico, but your family tells you not to say anything," Viri told me in our first interview, when I was writing about the Dreamer movement. Viri was preparing to take part in a civil disobedience action to protest the notoriously anti-immigrant sheriff of Maricopa County, Joe Arpaio. "I never knew what it meant to be Mexican. I thought it was something bad, so I decided I had been born in Phoenix. One day at school, all the kids were talking about what hospital they had been born in, and uh-oh, I didn't know what to say so I changed the subject, since I felt like it would be bad to say I wasn't from here."

Viridiana and I talked that day in the living room of her home, a house just like hundreds of others in West Phoenix, a Latino neighborhood. Her childhood and teen years were more or less un-eventful, until she reached the universal breaking point for Dream-ers: applying to college. She knew she was undocumented, but she found out what that really meant when she wanted to apply for college scholarships. When she got up her courage to talk to a school counselor, and for the first time in her life admit she was un-documented, the counselor told her not to waste her time because her parents certainly did not have $20,000—the cost of a year at college in Arizona at the time —and, anyway, what was the point of going to college if in the end you could not legally get a job?

Viridiana was devastated. She wondered why she had worked so hard, and even blamed her parents for bringing her to the US in the first place.

When she tells me this, Viridiana, of the strong presence, breaks down. She tries to hold back her tears as she tells me how sorry she is for having blamed her mother, and she repeats what her mother told her: she did it because the family had nothing in Mexico.

Viridiana tells me what hurts her the most: "My brother, who was born here and could go to any college he wants, he says he doesn't want to go to college." Viri sobs. "How can he not under-stand what he is giving up? I love him and I respect his decision, but I can't help but feel it's not fair. How come people who have the opportunity don't want it, and people who do want it have to fight so hard?"

In the end, Viridiana did find a way to go to college. With her mother's help, she found a private college near her home that helped locate private scholarships and other support from various organizations, so the bill Viridiana had to pay each year shrank. Her community also generously pitched in. While she was a high school student, Viridiana started offering free English classes to people in the area, with the goal of helping them understand their rights as undocumented immigrants. Her act of generosity came back to her in a way she never expected when her students, mostly adults, took up a collection and organized fund-raisers to help with her tuition costs. Viridiana graduated with honors in 2013, the first person in her family to graduate from college. She now works as the executive director of the Arizona Center for Neighborhood Leadership.[5]

The night Lupita García de Rayos was detained by immigration agents, dozens of activists gathered in front of ICE Enforcement and Removal Field Operations offices in Phoenix to protest. At least seven protesters were arrested for blocking the van that was transporting Lupita. But the deportation process carried on, and the following morning, after twenty-one years spent in the US, Lupita found herself back in Mexico. The last time she had been in the country, she was fourteen years old, the same age as Jacqueline, her daughter, who is two years younger than her brother Angel, sixteen. Her two children are both US citizens.

After Lupita's arrest, an intense social media campaign began demanding that her deportation be stopped. If, as Trump had said during his presidential campaign, people who had committed a crime or who posed a legitimate threat to national security would be prioritized for deportation, what was the point of tearing apart a hardworking family in Arizona?

Activists fighting for the García family asked Arizona Republican senator John McCain to intervene on Lupita's behalf. But that same day, Trump's spokesperson, Sofia Boza, said that by detaining people like Lupita, the president was fulfilling his campaign promise and targeting criminals first. Boza said Lupita qualified as a criminal for possessing false documents, which is a "serious crime" of "identity theft."

When she arrived in Mexico, Lupita decided to return to her birthplace in Guanajuato, in the middle of the country. She maintained contact with her children through long phone conversations, sometimes talking all night until dawn. Because they are American citizens, Jacqueline and Angel were able to visit their mother in April 2017 during their spring vacation. But Lupita's husband, who is undocumented and does not want his name to appear in print, cannot travel to Mexico. Now, with his restaurant job, he is the family's sole provider. Meanwhile, Lupita decided to start her own small business, and opened a tortilla shop in Acámbaro, a city in southern Guanajuato.

The future of the Garcías' marriage is uncertain. In an interview from Mexico, four months after she was deported, Lupita said she hoped a judge would reconsider her case, "but we don't know if I'll go back there someday, or if he'll come live with me," she told a reporter from the Spanish-language daily *La Opinión*.[6] "Because if he comes here, who's going to take care of our children, who want to go to college and have careers?"

CHAPTER TEN

LITTLE LEGS, BIG DREAMS

Mafalda Gueta, twenty-three
Guadalajara, Jalisco/Riverside, California

IN 1994, THE YEAR the Zapatista Army of National Liberation (EZLN) rose up in Mexico, the North American Free Trade Agreement (NAFTA) went into effect, and a Mexican presidential candidate was assassinated, Carlos and María Esther Gueta became the proud parents of twins, a boy and a girl they named Sebastian and Mafalda. As soon as they were born, Sebastian had to be treated for a congenital heart defect that impeded the flow of oxygen to his lungs. When the little boy had almost recovered from the surgery, the Guetas found that his sister also needed medical attention.

"When I was born, the doctors told my parents I would never be able to walk, or stand, or sit up," said Mafalda, "[that] I would be lying down my whole life."

Mafalda is short, with an oval-shaped face, brown hair, and an infectious smile. She looks like her father. She had long hair when I first met her. It was May 2015, and the University of California at Riverside (UCR), which Mafalda attended, was holding a banquet to raise funds for scholarships for undocumented students. Mafalda was the master of ceremonies. Wearing a white dress, black sweater, and Doc Martens boots, with a self-assured smile, she walked across the stage and proceeded to talk about her classmates and the struggle all undocumented students have to go through just to graduate. The crowd applauded, moved by her words.

In recent photos on social media, Mafalda has a radiant smile and is dressed in a graduation cap and gown. On her Facebook page, Mafalda describes herself as having "little legs, big dreams."

Mafalda had sacral agenesis, a rare condition that meant she was born without a sacrum, or lower spine. It not only affected her ability to move, stand, and walk; it also affected her internal organs, including the development of her bladder and intestines.

When the doctors gave them the diagnosis, Mafalda's parents started researching all the treatment options available, but there were none for children with this condition in Guadalajara, where they lived, or anywhere else in Mexico. (This was before the Children's Rehabilitation Centers, part of the Fundación Teletón, existed in Mexico, which now provide treatment for similar conditions.) At the time, Mafalda's maternal grandparents and an aunt lived in the United States. Mafalda's uncle found out about Shriners Hospital, which specialized in treating children with burns and spinal issues. Mafalda's mother immediately made an appointment for a consultation, and there the hospital told Mafalda's parents that surgery and further treatments were possible.

When the doctors at Shriners Hospital explained what the course of treatment would most likely be—several years of surgeries and follow-up consultations—Carlos and María Esther made the decision that any parent in the same circumstances probably would have made. They quit their jobs—he worked at a travel agency, and she worked for an airline, which was how they met—sold their house, withdrew the little savings they had left after Sebastian's and Mafalda's medical bills, and moved to Alta Loma, California, where their relatives lived. They arrived there in November 1995, just before Thanksgiving, on tourist visas. Mafalda and Sebastian were just one year old.

María Esther started working cleaning houses and did this for three years. It took Carlos a bit longer to find work, but he eventually landed a job at a travel agency. Mafalda started her medical treatment. At the same time, they tried to legalize their immigration status. María Esther's father was a US permanent resident and could petition for his daughter.

In 1995, María began the process of applying for legal residency, under the guidance of a Catholic organization that provided advice. To speed up the application, the organization suggested that María Esther say she was "single" on her application. Later, it would discover that was very bad advice: since she had entered the US on a visa stamped into her passport, and her passport said she was married, claiming she was single meant she had lied on her immigration application. Lying on the application is considered a federal crime. The Guetas then realized there was no way for them to legalize their status, at least not at that time.

By then Mafalda was receiving excellent medical care, with a greater chance of being able to walk one day. Shriners Hospital offers its services free of charge, regardless of a patient's or family's immigration status, to children from birth until the age of eighteen.[1] Mafalda had undergone her first surgery when she was two years old. By the time she was three, she had taken her first steps. There was a real likelihood that she would be able to walk if she kept up with the treatment protocol, so the family decided to remain in the United States, even though they would be undocumented.

When Mafalda was five years old, she underwent a completely innovative surgical procedure with a tongue twister of a name, appendicovesicostomy, also known as the Mitrofanoff procedure, in which a patient's appendix is used to create a conduit from the bladder to the skin's surface on the abdomen. For Mafalda, who had had to use a catheter to empty her bladder, because she could not control the muscles regulating urination, the conduit connecting her bladder to an exit point near her belly button changed her life, and the catheters were history.

"This procedure was totally new to many doctors. Shriners was doing things that were changing everybody's lives," Mafalda explained to me when we talked in 2017, a few days before she graduated from college. She spoke quickly and passionately. Emotion rose in her voice when she talked about the part her parents played in this process.

The Guetas had obviously come to the right place to address Mafalda's physical condition. But as her treatment progressed, there were some problems in terms of her social development. When their daughter reached school age, Carlos and Esther decided to send her to a special school for disabled students, with staff trained in how to work with and support children with conditions like Mafalda's. Later on, though, they decided Mafalda should be in a mainstream environment, which she would have to navigate for the rest of her life. At seven years old, Mafalda was enrolled in a general-education public school, and that was very hard for her.

Accustomed to being treated no differently from anyone else, Mafalda suddenly found herself in a place where the teachers did not know how to manage a student like her, and they had no training to help them deal with the mental and emotional effects of working with a disabled child. As a result, Mafalda's mother often had to intervene on her behalf. Once, when Mafalda had to empty her bladder—something she could not do in the same way as all the other students—the school nurse refused to help her, because she did not know how.

"I could not do it on my own, and she refused, and by refusing she was putting me in danger. My mom was really mad. She talked to the principal and the superintendent. She made everyone make adjustments and made sure the nurse and my teachers knew how to manage my situation. After that, the nurse was usually really nice to me. You don't know what goes on in the adult world, and I don't remember that much about how things got done, but my mom was like that; she acted like a mom. She literally left her country so that I could get the care I needed. When it was necessary she fought with doctors, with teachers; whatever she had to do, she did it. The nurses thought she was really aggressive," Mafalda remembers with a laugh. "She thought since she only spoke Spanish they were going to take advantage of her. My mom is really sweet, but if you mess with her kids, watch out."

Later Mafalda would make clear that did not mean her mother was overprotective, a natural response for anyone who loved her. Her grandparents, for example, were always saying, "Mafalda shouldn't do that." She remembers once her mother asking her to wash the dishes, and her grandparents said she shouldn't do that. María Esther responded, "Why not?"

"I think my disability could have been a weakness, but my mom turned it into a strength," Mafalda says. "She never made me feel like a weak person, because she knew someday I would have to do things for myself. My parents always pushed me to be independent. Some people want to help you because they care about you, but that help can sometimes make you too dependent. She didn't allow that, and that helped me to be a leader, because she pushed me to do things that were hard, even if it took me a long time. It's more work for me to do some things because of my disability, but I don't let myself think it will be difficult."

For the past two years I have kept in contact with Mafalda and her family through social media. Seeing the personal stories and events they share, it is easy to understand the ties that bind the Gueta family. Mafalda's father, Carlos, likes to post about the accomplishments and daily lives of his three children, the twins and their little sister, Enola, who is now fourteen. Music lover that he is, Carlos goes to lots of concerts—one of the advantages of living in the Los Angeles area—and often brings Mafalda along. A few weeks before my conversation with her, the whole family had gone to see the folk-punk band Violent Femmes.

"I'm very proud of my relationship with [my family]," Mafalda says. "They have always been close to us [kids], wanting to know what things we like, to understand us. How many moms do you know like anime?" Mafalda says, clearly touched by her mother's interest. "They've taught us how to keep ourselves safe and take care of ourselves; we don't hide things from them. My dad took me to my first concert when I was eleven. We went to see Green Day. We're friends on Facebook and connect through music and art. With my mom, it's anime and books. They are very modern and decided to grow along with us, so we have a friendship."

Her close family bond has no doubt been an important support for Mafalda during the difficult times in her treatment, and there have been many. Over the course of her twenty-three years, she has undergone thirteen surgeries, some with long recovery periods. When she was in kindergarten, Mafalda missed three months of school because of a surgery, and she missed three months again in fourth grade. Most of the surgeries were performed in her childhood years, because the main "problem" she faced was that she was still growing, and as long as she was growing, adjustments had to be made to her bone structure. She remembers one surgery made a chronic limp even worse. The medical team discovered that as her body had developed, one of her feet had grown in the wrong direction. They had to do an additional surgery to rotate her tibia.

"But once you stop growing, it's no longer a problem," Mafalda tells me happily. "I have lived alone, on my own, for three years now. I can say my parents did all they could to give us the best."

Norma speaks softly, almost in a whisper. At eighteen, she sounds like she doesn't want to call any attention to herself. She goes to school, works, and tries to live her life like any other young person her age; but she always has a dark shadow of fear over her. If her friends do anything that might attract the attention of the police, she gets nervous. She avoids going to certain areas and doing certain things. Norma is undocumented, and for as long as she can remember, she has lived with the knowledge that at any moment she could be identified by authorities, arrested, and deported.

This is the daily reality for the eleven million undocumented people living in the United States. It has an especially strong impact on young people whose options are severely limited at a critical juncture in their lives: they reach legal adulthood at eighteen, and as they try to plan for their futures, they find that every decision they make—going to school, working, traveling, driving a car—is limited because of their undocumented status.

In response to the hard reality thousands of young people in their communities faced, in 2015—the year I met Mafalda—a group of young researchers carried out a study entitled "Undocumented and Uninsured" to determine how the constant worry caused by their undocumented status takes a toll on the physical and mental health of undocumented youth. The results were enlightening: seven out of every ten study participants lack access to health care, although the same number say they need it. Of those who have an illness or a condition, half said they do not go to the doctor because they do not have health insurance, or for fear of being questioned about their immigration status. Six of every ten said they use the internet as an alternative, to try to find information on how to self-treat their conditions.

To carry out the study, thirty-four researchers, under the direction of three coordinators of the Healthy California project, part of the Dream Resource Center at UCLA, interviewed 550 young adults between the ages of eighteen and thirty-two in the state of California. To get precise results, interviewees had to meet one condition: they had to be undocumented at the time, or they had to have been undocumented at some point in their lives.[2]

"What we find is that our situation has not changed in recent years," Alma Leyva, one of the study's coordinators, told me. "Even though some people are recipients of DACA, we still see that policies of policing, of vigilance, continue to shape our lives. People live their lives avoiding things out of fear of deportation, and that is reflected in health care."

Leyva stresses that young undocumented people in the United States do not seek medical attention for fear of being identified as undocumented, even if they are suffering from chronic pain or easily treatable illnesses. Often the pain and discomfort caused by these illnesses is not serious, but it can be chronic. The lack of attention over time can lead to more advanced conditions that will require more complex treatment. Little aches and pains are treated with home remedies. Preventative medicine is not commonly practiced. When symptoms worsen, those affected wind up in the emergency room, leaving with huge medical bills because they lack health insurance or other health-care coverage. Cases of families finding a hospital or medical program that will provide long-term treatment at little or no cost, without having to prove US residency, like the Gueta family, are few and far between. Data on undocumented youth in general put people like Mafalda in an exceptional category.

When I ask Norma when she had last been to a doctor, she cannot answer. She pauses and tries hard to remember when it might have been.

"Honestly, I don't remember," she says. "Maybe when I was five or six and I had to get vaccinated for school. I'm grateful I'm not sick, but I do have a lot of stress, and I think that's why I get headaches. I think it also has to do with not eating very much from all the pressure at school and my job. Then I feel dizzy or my head hurts, and I take a pill or try to find some kind of medicine on my own."

Norma is twenty-one, and in many respects her life has been similar to Mafalda's. Her family, also from Guadalajara, came to the United States when she was three years old. She still has not been able to legalize her status. Since Norma is a DACA recipient, she can pay lower tuition rates and not the extravagant rates charged to foreigners who cannot show legal residency or citizenship in the US.

"But it's not just the money. You'll always have this fear that all of a sudden they could take away what they're giving you," she explains. "Now, the laws allow me to go to school, but that could change at any time, and not knowing if I'll be able to finish my degree causes me a lot of stress. It's a stress that gets added on to all the other everyday stresses, when something could go wrong. If my friends are doing something weird that could raise suspicions, and a police officer comes along and questions us, they might get a ticket or something, but I could get deported to Mexico. It's a tension that's always with me."

Norma is not the only one living with this tension. The UCLA study found that 83 percent of those interviewed acknowledged that they "auto-monitor" during the day to avoid activities that might arouse the suspicion of the authorities—meaning, they live in a constant state of high alert, avoiding high-risk situations. They do not go to the doctor because they are afraid they will be asked for documents proving their residency, and they alter their behavior to avoid situations that would cost them more money. They live in survival mode. Over the long term, conditions that start out as stress or depression can develop into physical ailments for lack of treatment.

Norma has never received any kind of preventative health-care service and has never had access to mental health services. According to the Dream Resource Center study, of the 550 young people interviewed, only 27 percent said they had access to any kind of psychological or emotional counseling if they needed it; 30 percent said they had access to some kind of emotional wellness services, and only 19 percent said they were part of a group that provided support.[3]

"I usually keep things to myself, or I tell my sister; that's all I can do," Norma tells me. "I think being undocumented has made me always aware of my situation. My friends tell me their problems, but I don't know exactly what they think about immigration, and sometimes I feel overwhelmed, because even if they're trying to be understanding, they can't understand what it's like to live like this."

If Norma doesn't get much help outside her home, there is not much help to be had inside her home either. Since she and her entire family are undocumented, medical care is in short supply for everyone. That hard reality may be behind Norma's goal to try to get work improving the quality of life in communities like hers in urban environments after she graduates from college.

"We try to be really careful and not get into any trouble. When one of us gets sick, everyone else tries to help—we try to find over-the-counter medicine; we pray and hope everything turns out all right."

With no access to a doctor, the best option is a pill and a prayer.

When I bring up the issue of health-care access with Mafalda, she responds immediately and says she knows the treatment that she and her family have received is a privilege. Her doctor is aware of her immigration status and made arrangements for Mafalda to continue receiving care after she turns eighteen, which is normally when patients need to find other options, until shortly before she turned twenty-one.

"It was twenty years of service," she says about the treatment she received uninterrupted for two decades. "They fitted me for orthopedic devices, and I found out when I was a kid they cost four thousand dollars for a pair—I can't tell you how many of those I had. They gave me medications, and I had thirteen surgeries; I was in the hospital for months after some of them. Can you imagine how much money we would have had to pay for twenty years of treatment and thirteen surgeries? And we didn't have to pay a thing. But it's not just the cost; it's that the treatments they offer you can't get anywhere else. They're always on the cutting edge," she says about Shriners.

It's often the case that undocumented people who do not have access to some services because of their immigration status tend to appreciate those services all the more when they do get them, since they understand all too well what it means to go without them. That is part of an undocumented person's identity: the awareness that your immigration status is always there, and that means limitations.

Mafalda clearly remembers the day she had that realization. It was July 29, 2010, the day the law SB 1070 went into effect in Arizona, which made employing undocumented people a crime.[4] Mafalda's mother lost her job the same day. For ten years she had worked in the accounting department of a supermarket chain that had started in California and expanded to Arizona. She liked her job, and the owner of the business valued her work. As Mafalda's father, Carlos, told me once: the business owner understood the worth of undocumented labor. When the supermarket-chain owner had to fire his workers, he hired a lawyer and searched for ways to legalize their immigration status, but he discovered that for people in those circumstances, there are no options. In María Esther's case, the supermarket-chain owner felt so badly about having to let her go, he offered her financial compensation. The crippling blow of having to fire his workers, coupled with the financial crisis of 2008–9, meant that he had to shut down the supermarket chain.

Understanding the implications of being undocumented also meant understanding the limitations Mafalda and her brother, Sebastian, would face in going to college. Carlos and María Esther did not know that their children would have to pay the same steep tuition fees as foreign students because they were undocumented, nor were they aware that their children were ineligible for federal financial aid for the same reason. At the time, there was little information readily available on what financing options were open to undocumented students who wanted to go to college, even from education professionals responsible for providing that information. Mafalda's parents met with a school counselor who told them that their children simply could not afford to go to college. This blunt assessment, on top of the growing anti-immigrant sentiment in the United States, made the Guetas for the first time consider returning to Mexico. It was 2012.

But before going back, the family decided to exhaust all their options. Mafalda and Sebastian asked around at several colleges and universities, and the answer was always the same: no financing available. Sebastian felt beaten down, but María Esther insisted that Mafalda go and talk to the University of California Riverside. "If they say no there, we'll stop," Mafalda remembers her mother saying. Mafalda went to UCR and found someone in the administrative office who was able to advise her on how to get financial assistance.

"That changed my future," Mafalda remembers. "I decided to go to UCR because of that. My first choice had been Santa Barbara, but UCR definitely was the best option, because it has stronger roots in the community. We [she and Sebastian] could build a network with other undocumented people there without experiencing the xenophobia like some of my friends at other schools have had to deal with sometimes. The five years I have been there have been a privilege. I've had a really good relationship with the dean, and I made some connections; there's a support network that includes professors who help undocumented students. It's a safe, welcoming community."

At around this time, DACA went into effect, which finally made Mafalda and Sebastian eligible for federal financial aid. Mafalda, always very outgoing, honed her leadership skills and began working for the Undocumented Students Project at UCR. In 2014, she was chosen to teach science at Yale University in a summer program for high school students, and she returned for three more summers. On June 18, 2017, Mafalda graduated with a bachelor of arts degree. She plans to work in education.

But now comes the hardest part, Mafalda asserts, as she starts planning for her future outside the safety net provided by UCR. Her ideal plan is to get a master's in science education degree—the University of California at Berkeley and the University of Texas at Austin offer this program. At the same time, she has started searching for jobs at some universities. When we last talked, two weeks before her graduation, Mafalda had already sent in some applications, one to be a program coordinator for undocumented students and another for a job coordinating a Latino student center.

Before our last conversation came to a close, Mafalda remembered that on November 8, 2016, her family had an experience similar to what they had gone through in 2010. The night Donald Trump won the presidential election, Mafalda called her parents in tears. María Esther cried too, but Carlos said firmly, 'We're going to be okay.'"

Says Mafalda, "My parents told me: 'We've been undocumented for a long time. We lived through the Bush years. We've been through so much, and we've gotten through it; we'll get through this too.' Now my biggest worry is my parents, because under the new administration's guidelines, they can be easily criminalized. It's easy to minimize their struggle, what they have done to give us the life we have had. I am about to become an undocumented college graduate, and because of the 'good immigrant' narrative, that gives me some space to keep going forward. I'm grateful for this, but my parents don't fit that narrative, and they are the ones seen as criminals. I'm not worried about me; I'm worried about them. I know that because I went to college and earned a degree, I am seen as being of more value to society than they are, but because of all their hard work, they are much more valuable than a lot of citizens, because they've worked twice as hard to give their family what we needed."

As for herself, her circumstances have resulted in one less worry. When she was fifteen, she met Sarah, a US citizen and now her girlfriend of eight years. For a long time Sarah said they should get married so Mafalda could legalize her status. Mafalda refused at first.

"I didn't want to fall into that stereotype [of getting married to get a regular immigration status] but when Trump was elected, we realized we didn't have any other choice. We have been together for eight years. We did it in a rush, but we want to have a real wedding when we can pay for it. Now, the priority is for me to legalize my status so I can take care of my own situation and my parents."

According to US law, once Mafalda has legal residency, three years must pass before she can become a US citizen. Then, in 2020, she can petition for her parents. That process usually takes between six months and a year, so the earliest Carlos and María Esther could legalize their status would be in 2021. The alternative would be to wait until 2023, when Enola, the Guetas' younger daughter, turns twenty-one, at which point she could petition for them.

"My parents had a good life, good jobs, a family, health insurance, and they left it all in a second just for the chance to give us a better life," says Mafalda. "If Mexico had been more developed in terms of medical care, maybe we would not have had to come here; my parents wouldn't have to worry about what might happen to them in the future. But even so, seeing what's going on in Mexico now, I don't know if we would have had any other choice. I don't even think the problem is about the government; I think it's a collective issue that has been there for a really long time."

When I ask Mafalda if she thinks hearing a story like her family's, of struggle and sacrifice for a long-term goal, would move anyone who's in charge of immigration policies in the United States, she sighs.

"I know a lot of people who choose to ignore what is right in front of them," she says. "I'd rather educate people who are ready to learn and grown. I think it's been shown that he's not a person who thinks like that," she says, referring to Trump, "so I don't know if I'd be willing to waste my time on him, because I believe it would be just that, a waste of time. If I'm going to talk to somebody, I'd rather talk to a community that could support me, not to somebody who I don't matter to at all."

CHAPTER ELEVEN

THE FUTURE IS FEMALE

Ana Elena Soto-Harrison, forty-seven

Mexico City/Longmont, Colorado

YOU SEE THEM OUT IN THE STREETS, taking public transportation, cleaning the train stations, driving the buses. They're in the restaurants cooking, waiting on tables, washing the dishes, and sometimes they even own the restaurant. They work in practically every industry in the country, from the fields where our food is grown, to the hospitals where the sick are treated. In spite of this, they are still living in inequality.

One of every five women in the United States is Latina. By 2060, they are projected to make up one-third of the female population in the country. A quarter of female students in public schools are Latina; in states such as California, Texas, and New Mexico, the figure rises, with Latinas representing one-half of all school-age girls.[1] And of all the Latina women in the United States, 64 percent are Mexican.

Clearly, the future of Latinas in general, and those of Mexican origin in particular, is relevant to the future of the United States as a whole. But in terms of education, few Latinas make it to college: less than 8 percent of college degrees are awarded to Latina women in the US. Access to higher education continues to be a challenge, and as a result they face limited career options.

Ana Elena Soto recognized this, and as a Mexican in the United States, she got the right to work to reverse those limitations, one girl at a time. In February 2017, she succeeded in getting seven Mexican families to consider the possibility of their daughters pursuing a higher education after graduating from high school. Ana gave them information on financial aid, how to apply to college, how to get scholarships and counseling, and about other options in different areas. The following year, and every year after that, Ana will try to reach many more.

Ana met her husband, Easton Harrison, in Mexico City while Easton was there on business. One day as he was walking along Paseo de la Reforma, a pretty girl caught his eye—Ana Elena. They struck up a conversation and their friendship began. The friendship blossomed into a romance and later marriage.

The couple settled in Houston, Texas, because Easton's four children from a previous marriage lived there. They lived in Houston for four years, but because of Easton's job, they would move several times in the coming years. First they moved to Boise, Idaho, where they spent three years and welcomed the birth of their daughter, Rosana. Then they relocated to Sandy, Utah, where their son, Gabriel, was born. Their next stop was Sparta, New Jersey, where they stayed the longest, from 2004 to 2013. Finally, the Harrisons moved to Longmont, Colorado, where they have lived for the past four years. A small city of 86,000 residents, one-fourth of whom are Latino, Longmont is thirty-three miles from Denver, the state capital.

Ana's experience living in such different places across the US has given her a fascinating perspective and valuable insights into the country. Ana and I met decades ago when we went to the same school in Mexico City. I think of her as a warm, loving, cheerful person, with a quick sense of humor and a facility for connecting with people. In early 2017, after not having seen each other for more than twenty years—except briefly at a school reunion event—we got together in Los Angeles. Ana got out of her car with her family: Rosana, a pretty fifteen-year-old girl; Gabriel, tall for his fourteen years but still with the face of a little boy; and Easton, her "gringo" husband, tall like his son. They are all bilingual, and Ana talks to her children in Spanish. My old friend has the same bright smile I remember—she is full-figured, with the same curly hair as always and friendly hazel eyes. Her warmth is reflected in her family life.

"Houston was the hardest for me," Ana told me a few weeks later on Skype. "I had just left behind my job, my family, everything I had in Mexico, and moved into a small apartment, with no furniture, with a television, a bed, and nothing else, in a new country. My English was not very good, but I've always been very social, so the hardest thing was being at home," she said, referring to her life with few friends and before having children.

Ana remembers her first experience with discrimination in the United States, right there in Houston. One weekend she and Easton went out to dinner at an upscale seafood restaurant. They were seated at a table and started talking to each other in Spanish. A few minutes later, they noticed that the man sitting at the next table was visibly uncomfortable.

"I can't tell you if I felt angry or afraid or sad speaking my language and seeing the reaction on that man's face. Feeling like you don't fit in, that attitude of 'I don't like you speaking that language because you're in my country' in his body language, his expression, everything. I didn't make a scene, we just left. Easton supported me. He was going to say something, but I told him I just wanted to leave. I had to let him know what it feels like when you know you're not welcome, something he's never going to feel because he's Anglo."

Although that episode was painful, it was practically the only discrimination Ana faced in Houston. She says Utah and Colorado were similar, with hardworking people originally from Zacatecas and Durango, from rural areas and ranches in Mexico, with a basic level of education.

"In Utah, I met people who had crossed the border undocumented," she says. "I remember one woman who made a deep impression on me. When I met her, she said, 'Someday I'm going to have a pink Cadillac just like Mary Kay,' the line of cosmetics that gives a car away to its best salesperson. Twenty years later, she has her Caddy. She really did it."

Things were a bit different in Dover, New Jersey, where Ana made friends with a group that included many Mexican families but from a higher socioeconomic background than what she had seen in Utah or in other Mexican communities in the New Jersey area. Most of the Mexicans Ana became friends with were professional couples who had left Mexico for good job offers in the United States. Ana felt comfortable in this group, who were also raising their children with typical Mexican family values such as having strong ties with their culture and their family back in Mexico, cooking traditional Mexican cuisine, and celebrating holidays like Día de los Muertos to remember their ancestors.

"Dover has a strong, completely Latino neighborhood," she says. "That is where you go to wire money to Mexico, and you know it will get to your family there with no problem, or where you can go to the market and buy your *nopalitos*. And you know what makes these communities strong? Their kids play soccer at the YMCA and at the park with the Boy Scouts, and the families go to the church brunch on Sundays. I found a community there that really blended into US society. I suppose that's because it's near New York City, so New Jersey has accepted Italians the same as Puerto Ricans, Ecuadorians, and Salvadorans. There's an easier coexistence that recognizes your culture, your food, and in general sends the message that you are welcome there."

When the Eastons lived in Texas and Utah and her children were little, Ana found it challenging to work or participate in activities outside of raising her kids. But since she has been active all her life, when her children were a little older and they lived in New Jersey, Ana began volunteering at their elementary school, where Rosana was in fourth grade and Gabriel was in third. She thought that if she got to know the staff, maybe in the future the school might let her teach. When she presented them with her idea, the school accepted, and Ana began teaching Spanish. With ten classes in the school, the teachers devised a plan so each class could have two forty-minute Spanish lessons per week.

"It was amazing; it gave me a real ego boost," she remembers. "I realized I could do it. [The children] were very interested. They were so grateful and ready to learn. Children bring that sense of wonder they have to language too; they are surprised by what they can do. They start off saying 'Yo *puedo hablar español*,' 'I can speak Spanish,' even though they have no idea what they're saying!" She laughs. "I found they had a real hunger to learn."

Unlike what Ana experienced at the restaurant in Texas, Ana says neither she nor her children experienced any discrimination in the years she worked as a volunteer Spanish teacher at their elementary school in New Jersey. And as is often the case with children of immigrants, Ana's kids were able to use their bilingual skills to help others: Rosana was once called to the nurse's office at school so she could translate for a girl who only spoke Spanish.

Although Ana was not paid a salary for her work teaching, she could see that her students, their families, and other teachers truly appreciated the value of learning another language. When she announced that she would be moving to Colorado, many parents sent Ana messages of thanks, and she received over three hundred cards and letters from students.

"That says a lot, too, because the demand is there, but the school could not make a job offer," Ana emphasizes. "Rosana is proud that she can speak Spanish. This generation is very different from earlier generations that were not allowed to speak other languages. There is more openness. Swing states [neither overwhelmingly Republican nor Democrat] like Colorado are very flexible. You can make a difference there."

When Ana arrived in Colorado, she quickly met other mothers in her area. One of her neighbors invited her to participate in a group, the Philanthropic Educational Organization (PEO), an international organization with a mission to improve educational opportunities for women and increase their representation in culture and the arts.[2] "To make their mark," Ana explains.

Enthusiastic about PEO's work, Ana started participating right away and soon found a path to making her own mark with a particular group: girls from Mexican families in Longmont.

Latina women in the United States are in many ways a diverse group. The three largest subgroups of Latina women are: Mexicans, representing 64 percent, followed by Puerto Ricans and Central Americans, at 9 percent each. The sum of these three groups makes up more than 80 percent of all Latina women living in the United States, and overall they have lower levels of income and education than the general population, although other smaller segments of the group, like Cubans, at 4 percent of the Latina population, and South Americans, at 6 percent, tend to be a bit better off financially.[3]

This is important, because Latinas are not evenly distributed throughout the country. There are many more Latinas of Mexican origin in the Southwest, while in the Southeast, Latinas of Cuban and South American origin are strongly represented. The Northeast has higher numbers of Puerto Ricans and Dominicans: Dominicans make up 3 percent of all Latinas in the US, and in the Midwest, the dominant groups are Mexican and Puerto Rican.

Although the common language for all Latinas is Spanish, and the different nationalities share some cultural references, there have been important variables in immigration patterns in terms of when people arrived in the United States and the conditions under which they arrived. What motivates someone in Mexico to migrate is not the same for someone from El Salvador or Cuba, and US immigration law has different provisions for each country of origin. For many years, the "wet foot, dry foot" policy, which allowed people to stay in the country once they set foot on American soil, applied to Cubans. And for years, Salvadorans have had temporary protected status, while Mexicans are not even given the right to a hearing before a judge if they are apprehended at the border, because of a binational agreement allowing Mexicans to be immediately repatriated.

Considering these differences, it's only natural that not all Latina women share the same experiences, backgrounds, needs, or opportunities. But given the large percentage of Latinas who come from disadvantaged economic backgrounds, overall this group still has limited financial and educational resources compared with the general population. Even though some parents of Latina girls have great aspirations for their daughters in terms of getting a college education and achieving career success, young Latinas are the least likely to earn a college degree of any group.[4]

The gap in educational achievement between Latinas and girls of other ethnic groups can easily be explained by the poverty and social disadvantages Latinas experience: one of every four Latinas lives below the poverty line, and more than half are low-income. In 2014, to be considered below the poverty line, a family of four had to earn less than $24,000 per year. For people living in countries such as Mexico, El Salvador, and Cuba, that might seem like a fortune, but in some major cities in the US, that amount would barely cover the rent and utilities for a two-bedroom apartment. Nutritious food, transportation, childcare for working parents, clothing, medicines, and health care—not to mention books and educational materials—are unaffordable luxuries on such tight budgets.

Latino children are also least likely to attend preschool.[5] In 2012, 63 percent of Latino children ages three and four did not attend preschool, compared with 51 percent of white and African American children of the same age.[6] Considering all of these factors, many Latino children enter kindergarten with academic disadvantages compared to their peers from other ethnic groups.

Aside from a lack of early childhood education, the language issue can be another obstacle. Around half of all Latinas in the United States enter school with Spanish as their primary language. The problem is that in spite of this country's rich history of migration and the advances that have been made in this area—especially in southwestern states like California, where official materials are printed in several languages—in primary education, a lack of English is viewed as a problem that needs to be "fixed" and is said to impede the child's academic progress. This view fails to recognize children's abilities in their native language and consider them an asset.[7] While other children are learning the regular curriculum, many Latina girls are still learning English, on top of grappling with all the previously mentioned disadvantages.

In this context, Ana got involved with PEO and discovered how the group worked on community, health, and recreation issues, ran a meal delivery program for the homeless in the winter, and organized book groups. She was pleasantly surprised by how warmly she was welcomed into the group, and how everyone in it liked the fact that she was from Mexico. It wasn't long before a neighboring chapter of the organization told her it needed someone whose native language was Spanish to work on an education conference for girls going to college—a manual needed translation.

Ana hesitated, because even though her English is good, she was afraid some technical details in the manual might get lost in translation. But with Easton's help, and understanding this was important work, she took it on. The manual explained to parents how to apply for college loans and other forms of financial aid. Later Ana also translated the event's program and the questionnaires given out to participants to evaluate how the program went. It seemed only natural, then, that Ana join the outreach team to get Spanish speakers to attend the conference.

She loved the work. Ana had to give presentations to parents, especially mothers, explaining the conference's mission. Her first presentation took place at St. John the Baptist Catholic Church, where she attended services every week along with a large number of Latinas. Ana asked the church administration if she could hold an event there. The church agreed, and she gathered a group of forty young people and their parents one Wednesday evening, three weeks before the conference.

"I started off telling them we all want a bright future for our families, and we know that is related to our level of education," Ana says. "And if fathers and mothers get on the same page and think about building a career, there's opportunity for advancement. When you listen to teenage girls talk, they're talking about who's dating who, who are they going to marry someday—these are high school girls. And their parents . . . I don't know if it's because they're from rural areas, but they think about how they want a good husband for their daughter, a nice boy who doesn't drink too much. They're not thinking about a boy with a college degree. I think in some Mexican families, there's still this idea they have to make sure their daughters don't get pregnant out of wedlock.

Their goal is to have their daughter graduate high school, and if she doesn't get pregnant first, all the better."

Although Ana's assessment about the educational gap might sound harsh, statistics support it. Even though Latinas have made progress in rates of entering high school, after that the gap gets wider: one of every five Latinas between twenty-five and twenty-nine lacks a high school diploma, compared with one of every twelve women from other backgrounds. What's more, 36 percent of Latina women who did not finish high school say they dropped out because they got pregnant.

Progress has been made in higher education as well, but Latinas still lag behind other ethnic groups. In 2013, 19 percent of Latinas between twenty-five and twenty-nine years old had earned a college degree, compared with 23 percent of African American women, 44 percent of white women, and 64 percent of Asian American women. For advanced degrees, only four of every hundred Latina women had earned master's degrees, compared with 5 percent of African American women, 11 percent of white women, and 22 percent of Asian American women.

"At a certain point in the presentation, all the girls got very quiet," Ana remembers. "I said to them, 'I need to hear what you think, what are your priorities, your hopes and dreams.' They told me they wanted to finish high school and get a job at Kohl's, which isn't bad, but it made me realize that for them the highest goal is to finish high school, and after that whether they go on to college or not is a matter of luck. So I tried to steer the discussion towards what we want to do with our lives and what we can do with our lives. And if I tell them they could go to college, a lightbulb turns on. They say, 'If I could go, that would be great.'"

Ana's presentation was such a success, the girls got excited about going to the education conference and asked if they could bring their mother, their aunt, their godmother, and how much did it cost. The parents were also interested. As soon as Ana told them the conference was part of a movement of women supporting the advancement of other women who want to succeed in education and in business, the young women started asking questions.

What really worked for Ana during her presentations was sharing her personal story with the families. She told them she came from a different country, too, and that, upon arriving in the United States, she found a place very different from what she knew. She told the parents that she, too, had had to learn through her children how things were done: math might be the same here and there, but the system for teaching it in school is not the same. Ana had to re-educate herself through them. The college application and financial aid systems also work completely differently in the US from those in Mexico, and it seemed complicated to Ana. But thanks to this conference, Ana got to know other parents, and now she knew how to get things done.

The group in the church that day had an unexpectedly emotional response to Ana's presentation. Many parents acknowledged they were intimidated, because they themselves only went to school until sixth or seventh grade in Mexico. They asked Ana what they should do if they could not pay the $45 registration fee that day, but it was decided that the conference would waive the fee for ten low-income attendees, seven for families recruited by Ana. They thanked her for making the information available in Spanish.

The conference was held on February 25, 2017, at a community college in Longmont. There were forty-four attendees, including those recruited by Ana. Six speakers gave presentations in English and four in Spanish on topics including how to instill good habits for success in school, financial aid, security on campus, and how to cope with an "empty nest" when children go away to college. For the high school girls, there were talks on how to prepare for college interviews and how to have fun safely on campus.

"[The families] were so grateful, and you could see how eager they were to find out more; they wanted more for their daughters," Ana says. "The mothers are worried that their girls are growing up, that they already have boyfriends. They say things to me like, 'I've told my daughter if she wants to be a pediatrician, she has to work hard and forget about boyfriends.' These women are from Durango or Zacatecas; they come from small towns that they've left for their family. Some are single mothers, but they all want their daughters to go to college. They can see how an education could give them a different life. And I think many of these parents have not had the chance to really think about their children's future, so we are kind of one step ahead of them. And having the information in Spanish definitely makes them feel more comfortable—if this woman speaks my language, I can ask her anything. Even though some are bilingual because they've been living in the US for a long time, there is always more trust when you talk to someone who comes from the same place as you. The tone was, no one knows it all here, because we all come from a place where things are done differently. It's not just the language [we are learning]; it's also being a parent. No matter how many manuals there are, we're still learning all the time."

The comments Ana received after moderating and translating a workshop for parents at the conference were all expressions of gratitude. In the workshop, she emphasized that not everyone is cut out for college and that technical school can be a good option for some young people.

"You don't want to fall into the belief that if you don't go [to college], you won't go anywhere," Ana said. "One of the speakers talked about how she set up her beauty salon in a spa, because when her father told her he wanted her to continue her education, she decided she would study something she could finish quickly, so she could start her business."

Ana beams with satisfaction when she talks about the results of her participation in the conference, but she says she wishes more people could have attended. Her goal for the coming years is to increase the number of participants, and she had done an evaluation to see what improvements could be made. She now knows that more time should be devoted to talking with the parents of daughters who have only just started high school and are not prepared to decide on college. Ana's goal is to tell them, without disparaging anyone's job, that girls have a great number of options open to them as they begin to build their lives, beyond marriage or working as a salesclerk in a retail store.

"The great thing about the project is [that] in the future we can educate our people at churches and recreation centers, even at

Mexican restaurants," Ana says. "We can pull in those young people and make them aware that there is so much out there beyond high school."

The night of November 8, 2016, as the results of the presidential election came in and it became clear that Donald Trump was going to win, members of demographic groups that had been the target of the candidate's vicious attacks during his campaign began to feel how the next four years were going to weigh on them. Among all of them, one group of almost two million people became the most vulnerable: young undocumented immigrants, most of them Mexican, known as Dreamers.

These young people, who arrived in the United States as minors, were hurt by the disparaging comments Trump made in the months leading up to the election about their origins or immigration status: he disparaged them for being immigrants, for being Latinos, for being Mexicans, and some for being Muslims. But beyond insults, the Dreamers received a direct threat: DACA, the temporary protected status granted by the Obama administration, would be removed once Trump was elected. These young people would once again be left without access to higher education and in a legal limbo that would make them immediately vulnerable to deportation.

When I spoke with Ana about this four months after Trump took office, he still had not taken any action to cancel DACA. Political analysts agreed that the new administration would keep this up their sleeve until the right time came to use the issue as leverage while negotiating other difficult issues in Congress.

As congressional representatives and other elected officials play politics with the lives of millions of people, the fear of what could happen to anyone who is undocumented has put many people on edge.

"Now they're afraid. They're not paralyzed, but they are scared, in suspense," Ana said, talking about what she has observed in Colorado. She tells me a story as an example. "The couple who cleans our house don't give out their business cards to anyone anymore, because they're undocumented. They're afraid someone will find out they are working under a false Social Security number. The wife told me, 'We want to buy a house. We could pay a down payment in cash, but how are you going to build up any credit if you don't exist as a person? If you're a ghost who pays taxes and generates income, who's working, but has no options?' They are clinging to the hope that these next four years will pass quickly and that a friend will help them get their house, managing the paper-work. They have enough savings to start to build up some capital, but they're afraid that if they get caught in a raid and get deported, they'll lose everything."

Ana told me this couple has three daughters, all Dreamers. One is finishing up nursing school, knowing that if DACA is repealed, she will not be able to practice her profession. As someone who came to the US with a green card and legal permanent resident sta-tus, Ana despairs at the prospect of not being able to do anything to help this family.

"It's like these people live in a kind of submarine, underwater all the time. You can't see their faces or the color of their skin, and they're extremely hardworking. Once I asked her, 'Would you go back to Mexico?' And she said, 'No, our life is here, our grand-daughter, our history, part of our family is here. There's no going back.' This is how a lot of people live, and I don't know if I could dare to do it. It takes a lot of nerve to make your life in a different country and even more to do it undocumented. Trump needs to get closer to our community that he assumes he knows, but he doesn't know at all. It would be great if he could see things from our perspective, what our young people have to put up with in this country, and it's a lot. To understand how we live, our values; see our talents and give us a chance to shine."

CHAPTER TWELVE

LAWYER DREAMS

Daniel Rodríguez, thirty-one
Monterrey, Nuevo León/Phoenix, Arizona

DANIEL RODRÍGUEZ is an attorney specializing in immigration and family law. Although this is a common area of specialty among lawyers in the United States, especially in states along the Mexican border, Daniel's case is unique: as of May 2017, he was the only undocumented attorney in the state of Arizona licensed to practice law.

The struggle to make it into the courtroom and open his own law practice began when Daniel was just a boy. With a family history in two countries, like many immigrants, Daniel's family has lived on both sides of the border, shaping how they saw the world, and how the world saw them.

Although he knew from a young age that he wanted to practice law, the family's financial circumstances and certain laws in place posed a series of obstacles in the way of Daniel's dream. He decided to go to law school and, at the same time, clear those stumbling blocks from his path, for himself and for other binational young people who would come after him. Now, he works on their behalf to eliminate some of those obstacles in US immigration court.

Daniel's maternal grandmother was born in Texas, where some of his relatives still live. When he talks about his family history, Daniel—trim, with dark hair and a goatee, almond-shaped eyes, and a sharp gaze behind his glasses—explains his family is part of a group that, because they have lived there for centuries, did not cross the border. Rather, the border crossed them, an allusion to the 1845 annexation of Texas from Mexico. When his grandmother married his grandfather, the couple moved to Monterrey, in Mexico, and settled there.

Daniel's mother was one of fourteen children. She was the first girl in the family to graduate high school, before earning a certificate as a secretary and marrying Daniel's father. They had a troubled relationship, and one day Daniel's mother decided to leave with her children and go to the United States. She had a cousin living in Phoenix who knew what a hard time she was having and offered to help.

"It wasn't very planned. I don't remember any conversations about it," Daniel tells me, looking back. He was seven years old at the time. I got together with him and Luis Ávila, both activists, at the Fair Trade Cafe in Phoenix, which has become a gathering place for human rights defenders in Arizona. "We left on a weekend; we crossed the border. I don't remember much about crossing, except that for me it was like going on a hike, up over a mountain. That's all I remember."

When the family arrived in Phoenix, they moved into their cousin's garage. Daniel's mother went from having a house, a career, and her family nearby, to losing it all from one day to the next. She started working cleaning bathrooms and offices. She also had to deal with Daniel's rebellious behavior, as he deeply resented the sudden change in his life.

"I was always mad when I was a kid," he explains. "At first I took it out on my mom, because I didn't understand what was happening. I was angry with her for what I felt like she had done to me, what she had done to all of us—I had lost my toys, my friends, everything. Sometimes we would talk about it, and her answer was always, 'Focus on your studies and be a good boy.' I grew up in Phoenix like any other Latino kid, but I only started to understand what being undocumented meant in high school."

This phenomenon—of not understanding the implications of lacking documentation to legally live in the country until one is about to apply to college or get a job—is a constant for young people who arrived in the US at a young age and grow up like any other American child, focusing on their schoolwork and being "good" boys and girls. Until one day they find that even though they have done just as their parents asked, the doors of opportunity are closed to them.

While in high school, Daniel went to his guidance counselor and asked what he had to do to go to college, because he was in a difficult situation: his mother had suffered a back injury at her new workplace, a meatpacking plant, and could not move. Daniel knew he had to do something to help out his mother, and of course, he remembered the message he and all the other kids had gotten: if you go to college, you can achieve the American Dream. When he told the counselor about his immigration status, however, she responded brusquely: "People like you can't go to college."

"I said, 'Oh, well, okay.' I was a sophomore in high school, and I decided then that I would get a job. There was a restaurant right next to the high school. I went in and said, 'I need a job. Do you have anything?' They said they needed a dishwasher, so I filled out an application. The manager interviewed me and asked for my Social Security number. I said, 'What's that?' He said, 'You can start tomorrow.'" Daniel laughed. "It was no problem."

Daniel started working and eventually decided he was going to drop out of high school. If his own guidance counselor had told him he couldn't go to college, why stay in school? It would be better to work and help his family. At that point, in what he describes as a "divine intervention," another guidance counselor at the school, Donna Bartz, came on the scene and changed his life. It was 2002.

"She told me she knew about our situation," he says. "The DREAM Act . . . had been introduced over a year earlier, and the subject was getting more attention. She asked me if I wanted to go to college, and when I said yes, she offered to help come up with a plan. She told me to work on my school record and that I should get involved in all the extracurricular activities I could, and [that] I should do community service and volunteer work."

Daniel started his junior year and followed Bartz's advice. He was the president of MEChA (Movimiento Estudiantil Chicanx de Aztlán), a Mexican American student organization with local chapters in states across the country; he was the president of both the Latin American Club and the Black Student Union. He also began writing for the school newspaper. In one of his first stories, Daniel wrote about attending a session of the Arizona legislature in 2003 in his capacity as president of the Black Student Union. There he had the opportunity to interview Leah Landrum Taylor, the only African American representative in the state's lower house. Landrum Taylor talked about a group of people who had been, as Daniel said, "tricked" into coming to the United States and were forced to work, who were mistreated all of their lives and were still fighting to be considered full citizens of the US with all of the rights of citizenship.

"I heard that story and I thought, 'That's my story, my family's story, my people's. It's my story,'" Daniel tells me, emotional. "And that's when I started to see my story as a Dreamer not through MEChA or the pro-immigrant movement; I discovered my story as a Dreamer through the history of African Americans in this country."

Daniel kept on working while preparing to go to college, and he started getting involved in immigration issues. He remembers that, in 2004, Ernestina Reyes, the MEChA faculty advisor, told him he had to be prepared because hard times were coming to the undocumented community. "They need people like you, who are out there, involved, leaders," she said. Daniel took her advice. He won a Fulbright scholarship and secured another private scholarship so he could afford college. In his first year at Arizona State University (ASU), the immigration issue was center stage: President George W. Bush had launched his campaign for reelection, and from Mexico, there was outrage over the epidemic of women murdered with impunity in Juárez City.

This was all preparation for what was to come in 2006. That year, Arizona passed Proposition 300, a measure prohibiting students who could not prove citizenship or legal residency in the US from receiving state or federal financial aid for college. What's more, they would be required to pay the same exorbitant tuition rates as foreign students. On top of this, Daniel's beloved teacher, Ernestina Reyes, died. When Daniel learned of his mentor's death, the hurt and anger he felt as a child resurfaced, and he decided to channel it for a good cause.

Daniel started going to meetings of activists who already had years of experience organizing the community around immigration issues; he listened to everything but did not participate very much in the discussions. When he went to the meetings, he noticed he was the only person under thirty in the room and the only undocumented immigrant; no one else from his generation was involved. He also became involved with the Somos America Coalition, which organized the massive pro-immigrant marches in 2006 in major cities such as Los Angeles, Chicago, and Phoenix. But even there, he felt somewhat frustrated by the lack of colleagues his age. "I thought, 'Where are my friends? Why aren't they here?' Then I decided I was going to organize students like me."

Daniel had his chance when Proposition 300 went into effect and many undocumented ASU students lost their financial aid. Together with some of these students, in 2008 Daniel founded the Arizona Dream Act Coalition (ADAC), which is still active.

When ADAC first started holding regular meetings, Daniel noticed that participants were focused on the fight for comprehensive immigration reform. But it was clear to him from the beginning that they needed to build a movement of young people and start telling their story of struggle for the DREAM Act.

"So I began telling my story as a Dreamer at events, in interviews, saying that I was undocumented, and if they wanted to, they could come arrest me. We did 'coming out' events in the legislature. We created a platform to tell our story publicly and to recognize our history, something that had not been done very much before," Daniel recalls. He refers to this movement as "coming out of the shadows," in which undocumented youth publicly declare their immigration status to affirm their right to stay in the country legally and pressure legislators to pass a law to that effect.

In 2008, as the Dreamer movement got stronger, a contentious contest for the Democratic Party's nominee for the presidential election in November of that year was under way. Barack Obama, a junior senator from Illinois and the underdog candidate, faced off against political veteran Hillary Clinton, building his grassroots campaign around a theme of "change" and relying on enthusiastic young volunteers known as "Obama's army." It's interesting to note that many of the Dreamers who began organizing to defend their right to an education also invested their energy in the winning campaign for the country's first African American president.

Daniel was one of those Dreamers. A friend of his, a lawyer who worked for the Phoenix city government, invited Daniel to attend a meeting where presidential hopeful Obama was going to give a speech. Daniel was very impressed by Obama's ability to communicate effectively and show empathy, emphasizing stories of real people he had met. Daniel joined his campaign through the university group Young Democrats.

That year, 2008, Daniel also entered law school, his dream since he was a little boy. But because of new laws passed by the state legislature and the economic crisis then roiling the nation, at the end of the first year, he lost his two scholarships. He would have to somehow scrape together more than $40,000 for annual tuition, living expenses, and his contribution to household expenses. Continuing law school became financially impossible. So Daniel decided to put his dream of being a lawyer on hold and devote his time and energy to activism and join the Dreamer movement.

The same year Daniel had to drop out of law school in Arizona, in California, a young man named Sergio García, thirty-two years old, took the bar exam, which law school graduates must pass in order to be licensed to practice law in their state. Sergio passed the exam on the first try; that year, only 49 percent of the aspiring lawyers taking the exam passed it.[1] But a few weeks later, that license was revoked because of his immigration status: Sergio was undocumented.

The García family emigrated from Mexico to the United States when Sergio was just one and a half years old and went back to Mexico when he was nine. When Sergio was seventeen, he returned to California. His father, a farmworker, applied for a green card—permanent resident status—on his son's behalf in November 1994. The federal government approved the application in 1995, one year before a federal law was passed stipulating that state agencies cannot grant professional licenses to anyone in the country illegally.

That should not have applied to Sergio, since his application met all the requirements for permanent resident status. But it's not that simple: given the enormous backlog of cases in US immigration court, the fact that Sergio was informed his citizenship application would not be approved until approximately 2019, ten years after his graduation, was unsurprising. So, along with thousands of others in the same situation, he was in a legal limbo that, among other things, prevented him from practicing the profession he had worked so hard to enter.

Sergio decided that if ever there was a time to put what he had learned in law school into practice, it was now. In early 2013, Sergio García, representing himself, appeared in the California Supreme Court in, literally, the case of his life: arguing for his right to keep his license to practice law.

Sergio's case attracted the public's attention. On the one hand, the academic institutions where he had studied, California State University at Chico and Cal Northern School of Law, as well as the State Bar of California, considered him competent to practice law. On the other hand, Sergio's case highlighted the woeful deficiencies of the bureaucracy in managing US immigration and the injustice caused by applying legal criteria that have nothing to do with the individual realities of those living in the country. The case got my attention too. Over the days it was litigated, I got in touch with Sergio to find out more about his story.

Sergio talks like a lawyer, choosing his words with care. "I'm at a very dramatic point," was the first thing he said as we began talking. "Unfortunately, the court acted in a very cowardly way when it said they could not do anything unless the California legislature opens the door. Okay, God willing, the legislators will support us."

Sergio was referring to the response he got from California's Supreme Court when he presented his case. When he passed the bar exam in 2009, the State Bar of California submitted an application for a license to the court on his behalf, as a matter of routine procedure. But once they identified his immigration status, the authorities in charge of granting licenses decided to review it further.

The federal law that explicitly prohibits granting licenses to anyone without legal immigration status meant that he would not get a favorable ruling, Sergio was told during court proceedings. The only way to bring about a different outcome would be a state law specifically establishing the legality of granting a professional license to someone regardless of immigration status. Court adjourned, and a verdict in his case was to be delivered within ninety days.

Sergio was driving in his car as we talked on the phone. He was on his way to a California assemblyman's office to continue the work he had been doing before arguing his case in court: mobilizing as many state politicians as possible to make the legal changes necessary to win his case, before the court rendered its verdict.

The young lawyer had already demonstrated his effective negotiating skills when, on September 6, 2009, a few hours after his appearance in court, Democratic assemblywoman Lorena Gonzalez presented measure AB 1024 to the state legislature, with the support of all the Latino representatives. If passed, the measure would amend Section 6064 of the Business and Professions Code relating to attorneys, allowing the state supreme court to admit an applicant not lawfully present in the United States as an attorney-at-law in all the courts of the state, "upon certification by an examining committee that the applicant has fulfilled the requirements for admission to practice law." A few hours before the measure came up for a vote, Sergio was busy convincing the legislators.

"I've explained to them that I only have a year to get this resolved, because the results of the bar exam are valid for just five years. I explained this was an emergency for me, and it's practically a miracle they've responded so quickly. In just a few hours, the initiative will be ready to be voted on, to defend my American Dream," he said.

On September 12, the initiative was passed, with sixty-two votes in favor, four votes opposed, and two abstentions. It next landed on the desk of California governor Jerry Brown, who signed the measure into law on October 5. The law went into effect on January 1, 2014, clearing away any obstacle for the court to grant Sergio his license to practice law. A month later, Sergio became the first undocumented attorney allowed to officially practice in the United States.

Until then, a case similar to Sergio García's had never come up in any other state court, making the resolution a precedent for other cases in years to come. Sergio had several teams of lawyers around the state fighting for him, around 150 people in total. The days after his case was decided were a whirlwind for Sergio. While messages of congratulations and solidarity poured in from colleagues and friends, he fielded interview requests from the press, and was even invited to appear on *The Daily Show* with Jon Stewart. When I talked to him, Sergio said around half of his supporters were non-Hispanic white citizens.

"I think the first thing this case shows is that immigrants aren't just groundskeepers, cooks, or construction workers—which are all honorable, fine professions—but we're also professionals who want to work. We are qualified and have a dream to fulfill," Sergio said. "We don't know how many more young people have graduated law school or medical school with no possibility of practicing. It is hypocritical on the federal government's part to praise young undocumented immigrants who want to pursue an education but then prevent them from getting a license," he added in a reference to President Obama, who expressed his support for a law granting undocumented youth legal status throughout his eight years in office. "They should let us know what they really intend to do with us."

After three years of activist work, Daniel Rodríguez started thinking about how he could go back to law school. According to the
school's regulations, if he did not reenroll that year, 2012, the one
year of law school he had completed would no longer be valid.
The challenge was still getting enough money together to pay for
it. Then he got an idea: since it was an election year, dozens of
candidates for office were holding campaign fund-raisers, asking
for contributions with the promise to serve their community once
elected. Daniel thought, "If I have a dream, and part of my dream
is to support my community, why can't I have a fund-raiser for my
education?" He talked it over with his friend Luis Ávila, who he
had worked with for several years in social activism.

"I said to Luis, 'I've wanted to be a lawyer ever since I was
seven years old,' and he said, 'That will be the name of your campaign: Ever Since I Was Seven.' I started the campaign. I launched
a website that is still online. I threw parties on the weekends. I got
together with people my friends invited in cafés, just like a political
campaign. It was structured just like a political campaign, but for
my education. And at the same time, when I began my campaign, I
got involved in Obama's [reelection]. I noticed every time I wanted
to go to school, Obama wanted to be president!" he says with
a laugh.

In 2008, immigrant rights activists had supported Obama's
campaign in the hopes that he could get favorable immigration
reforms passed. In 2012, the motivation was to ensure the defeat
of his opponent, Mitt Romney, who not only would make no progress in this area but whose election could mean a serious setback.
Even though in his first term in office Obama was unable to fulfill
his promise to the immigrant community of passing immigration
reform, or at least the DREAM Act, people like Daniel rejoined his
campaign to make sure the few protections undocumented families
had would stay in place.

On November 6, Election Day, Daniel was busy studying for
his final exams, so he could not participate in any campaign events
that day. But he remembers the moment the results were announced

and Obama was declared the winner. As polling places across the country closed, Obama's campaign team, volunteers, and supporters in Arizona waited for the results to come in at a hotel in downtown Phoenix. Daniel headed to the hotel that night, taking a bus downtown and listening to the election results on the radio.

"They were announcing the states, and only Ohio was left, the state that would decide the election. It was just the bus driver, me, and a young African American guy on the bus. I was listening; they were about to announce the results, and I wanted to cry—I'm such a political nerd," he says, laughing. "I was alone; all my friends were at the hotel already. So I went over to the other guy on the bus, because I didn't want to be alone in that moment, and I said, 'Hey, do you want to listen to what's happening with the election?' He gave me a weird look, but I said, 'Listen, they're going to say who won for president!' Then I gave him one of my earphones, and the two of us heard them say Obama had won. When I got to the hotel, everybody was crying."

Daniel graduated from law school in 2014, and then the battle to get a license to practice began. Along the way, because this has always been his approach, he formed a group of Dreamers at his law school, calling themselves the Dream Bar Association. They were all prepared to fight for their licenses in their respective states.

"I thought, 'I'm in Arizona; they're not going to give me one.' But I graduated, and I had my legal team ready to go to court and argue for my license, and in October I got the approval notice in the mail. I don't know how, that's just what happened. The great irony is, they gave me a license to practice law, but I still could not get a driver's license, so I would go to court looking very professional but without a driver's license," he says with a laugh. As of now, Daniel is the only undocumented lawyer in the state.

In 2015, together with his business partner Otilia Díaz, Daniel opened a law office that employs three other people and has created two free legal clinics to counsel immigrants. Daniel left the volunteer work to other organizations—over the course of the ten years since he first began his activist work, community and

activist groups have multiplied. Daniel did not see himself as in-
dispensable. Still, he wanted to find his place in the pro-immigrant
movement.

He discovered his place in the movement in November 2016.
On Election Day, not only would the race for president be decided but voters would also go to the polls across the country to
elect congressmen, governors, mayors, and sheriffs—including the
feared sheriff of Maricopa County, Arizona: Joe Arpaio.

For twenty years, Arpaio, who liked to call himself "America's toughest sheriff," waged a campaign against undocumented
immigrants in the county, which includes the state capital of Phoenix, with the goal of driving them out. Arpaio loved publicity and
proudly promoted a campaign of relentless persecution, even appearing on three episodes of a Fox TV reality show called *Smile . . .
You're Under Arrest*, in which he was shown (of course) arresting
immigrants.

Because of Maricopa County's location near the Mexican border and Arizona's large immigrant population—representing 15
percent of the state, and mostly from Mexico—it is easy see why
Arpaio would be extremely popular with anti-immigrant groups
like the Minutemen vigilante group and with powerful conservative politicians, mostly white. These supporters justified the relentless human rights violations committed by Arpaio's officers when
they arrested people who had committed no crime but were in the
country undocumented—a function that is the responsibility of the
federal government, not the Sheriff's Office.[2]

That support was reflected at the polls for a long time. Arpaio
was reelected again and again, always winning around 60 percent
of the vote. With that endorsement from the public, he trained his
officers in harassing immigrant communities, without respect for
legal procedures designed to protect everyone in the country and
ensure that local authorities do not function as federal immigration agents. In Arpaio's domain, people walking or driving around
who looked Latino could be stopped for any reason—for a broken
taillight or "suspicious behavior"—and asked for documentation

proving legal US residency. If they could not provide it, they would be arrested and put into deportation proceedings.

But in the later years of his tenure, support for Arpaio declined. Between 2004 and 2007, almost 2,700 lawsuits were filed against him, in courts in Maricopa County as well as federal courts, for civil rights violations and for unlawful stops and arrests based on racial profiling, among other charges. In April 2008, Phoenix mayor Phil Gordon asked the US Justice Department and the FBI to formally investigate Arpaio, and in 2011 the Justice Department and a federal court revoked the sheriff's authority to identify and arrest undocumented immigrants. In 2012, the Justice Department filed its own lawsuit against Arpaio for continuing to practice racial profiling and unlawful discrimination—he had not altered his department's methods in the slightest.

In this context, the election on November 8, 2016, was very important for Maricopa residents. Though Donald Trump won his bid for the White House, Joe Arpaio, one of Trump's staunchest allies, lost his reelection bid to an intense activist campaign, bringing a twenty-four-year reign of fomenting terror among immigrants to an end.

"That night, which should have been a celebration for us in Arizona for winning, for getting rid of Arpaio, I cried," Daniel tells me, remembering the sense of helplessness he felt. "We were watching results come in from the presidential election, and it was so sad. . . . But in that moment, all of the unrest, that passion I felt since I was a little kid, since 2005, since 2010, came back, and I said to myself, 'We have to do something.' It was frustrating because everyone I talked to after the election didn't know what to do, but to me it was obvious we had to change things. I think some people are still organizing and thinking as if we're still under the Obama administration, but no, everything's changed."

A few days later, Daniel met his friend Luis at the Fair Trade Cafe. It was early in the morning, because Daniel had to be at court at eight o'clock. They got together to talk about their plans for the future. They had to try to stop the policies Trump would probably enact, using a resistance strategy similar to what Arizona had done to resist them. In Daniel's mind, Trump was the country's Arpaio. They remembered one of their biggest activist successes, the "Boycott Arizona" campaign, and began planning how to launch something similar but on a national level and involving Mexico, the state's vilified next-door neighbor.

But that's another story.

CHAPTER THIRTEEN

BOYCOTT

Luis Ávila, thirty-five
Culiacán, Sinaloa/Phoenix, Arizona

IN JULY 2010, SB 1070, the law criminalizing undocumented immigrants and anyone who provided certain services, such as housing, to them, went into effect in Arizona. Daniel Rodríguez and Luis Ávila decided an appropriate response would be to organize a boycott against the state of Arizona.

The concept sounded far-fetched. Who would want to boycott the very state they lived in? But Daniel and Luis's reasoning was simple: if you don't want to recognize our community's worth—the "you" here referring to conservative authorities and anti-immigrant groups—then we'll hit back where it hurts the most: at businesses and your wallets.

Support for the boycott, which was strongest among potential event attendees and visitors to tourist destinations in Arizona, resulted in a loss of $600 million in state revenue. The valuable lessons in strategy learned from that experience were ingrained in the two activists who had conceived of the boycott, and the opportunity to put them back into practice presented itself in November 2016.

When Donald Trump won the presidential election, Daniel and Luis, now with even more experience under their belts, decided to create a similar strategy. They wondered, What would happen if we asked Mexico to boycott US corn?

Luis Ávila was born in Culiacán in 1982, but he barely remembers anything about Sinaloa. When he was very small he moved with his parents to Tijuana, where he spent most of his childhood. He went to elementary school there, while his father worked in a bank and his mother in a department store. His sister was born there, and as often happens in families along the border, his brother was born in the United States.

A few years later his father, whom Luis describes as "one of those men who gets ideas," decided to start his own business. Using savings and some loans, he bought some land in Bajío, a region in central Mexico, and started a dairy farm. The family moved to Mexico City for a year and then to the city of Querétaro, which was closer to the little village called Doctor Mora, in Guanajuato, where the dairy farm was. Twelve years old at the time, Luis would go to help out on the weekends.

When talking about his father's attempts at running a business, Luis uses a less than politically correct metaphor to explain how it always goes wrong: if he were to buy a circus, the dwarfs would grow tall. Just when Mr. Ávila bet it all on milk production, Mexico reached an agreement to buy powdered milk from the US, and domestic milk prices plummeted. The cost of producing the fresh milk that most Mexicans used to consume—in bottles, not in Tetra Paks, or powdered, which they buy now—became very high in relation to the consumer price for the product, so Luis's father's business began to fall apart. First, he sold off some cows and scrambled for alternatives. He applied for more loans and decided to grow broccoli instead. But then the price of broccoli fell dramatically, too. He lost land, until he was left with just a small plot that could not be used for much.

When Luis graduated high school, he had the chance to go to the United States to learn English. By that time, the family was experiencing such financial trouble that they couldn't cover basic expenses such as rent or school fees for Luis and his siblings. Luis's mother started going to the United States for short periods to work. She got temporary jobs driving a taxi or cleaning houses, and then would go back to Mexico, bringing home her earnings to pay the bills or buy clothing for the children, while their father tried to climb out of the financial hole he had dug.

"That caused problems between them; there were fights," Luis says. "My dad started drinking. He became more violent, and our nuclear family was broken. My mom was working a lot. I was seventeen, and I got a small scholarship to study English. So I took the opportunity and came here one summer, assuming I would go back to Mexico to enroll in college."

That was the plan initially. But once Luis was in Arizona, he decided to experiment a little: what would happen if he applied to college there? Without giving it much more thought, he completed and submitted an application to Arizona State University. Then, much to his surprise, he was accepted.

"I was the first person in my family to go to college, so to them, being accepted to an American university was like I had gotten into Harvard," Luis says with a laugh. "Everyone said it was an opportunity I couldn't pass up. And I was really lucky, because when my dad was really young he had gone to Oregon to work, and he benefited from the 1986 amnesty. At that time, he applied for legal residency for me, and eighteen or nineteen years later, I got my green card, just in time to come to the US."

By then Luis's parents were separated, so he and his mother and siblings began making plans to move. On July 31, Luis's birthday, he rode a bus to go live with one of his aunts. The others arrived later, and his mom started working driving a shuttle bus between Nogales and Phoenix.

But one important detail Luis and his family did not know was that since he was not a resident of Arizona, he would have to pay out-of-state tuition—three times more than what state residents paid. So Luis also had to get a job to pay for college. Like many immigrant families, Luis's family did not speak English, and they all got jobs in the service sector, sometimes working more than one. Luis's first job was in a Peter Piper Pizza, cleaning. Later he had a job in a Jack in the Box, and also worked preparing food for private events.

Luis worked for five years so he could go to college. Some semesters he could only afford the time and money to take a single class. Although he did receive some financial support for tuition after the first year, Luis still had to cover his other living expenses. His family also depended on the income he earned, since his mother did not make enough to support four people.

"We didn't have a car; we had to take the bus. Everything cost money," he says. "Little by little, we got on our feet. We moved into an apartment where we lived for several years, and later I moved out to live closer to the university. Things started going better for my dad in Mexico, so he started helping us out a little financially. While all this was happening, my two brothers and I graduated college."

Luis decided to study journalism and Latin American literature, and soon he founded a bilingual magazine at the university. That's how he met Daniel Rodríguez, who would become his comrade-in-arms not only at school but in activism too. And like Daniel, during his years in college, Luis learned all about social issues and politics in the United States.

In that time, Luis also met several undocumented students who told him they could not go to college. It was hard for Luis to believe that he could come to the US and have access to a higher education while other young people who had grown up here could not. This was before anyone had started talking about the DREAM Act and the Dreamers themselves, but Luis got involved with other movements and issues: migratory politics, opposing initiatives to make English the official language of Arizona, and organizing resistance to other anti-immigrant proposals. Along the way, a generation of young activists rose up and came together to create a network that has successfully fought some measures, including the controversial anti-immigrant legislative initiative SB 1070.

On the morning of April 23, 2010, Arizona entered a time machine. With the stroke of a pen, Governor Jan Brewer signed SB 1070 into law and sent her state careening back to the early twentieth century, when the territory first joined the Union as Arizona. Before that, it had been Mexican territory, inhabited by Native American tribes including the Pueblos, Yaquis, and Navajos. Brigham Young, leader of the Church of Jesus Christ of Latter-day Saints, or Mormons, decided to populate the area with white people of European descent. Under that premise, cities such as Phoenix, Tempe, and Prescott, the heart of the present-day state, were formed.

For a century, the quest to establish white dominance has marked Arizona as a state with the most regressive, racist politics in the country. Some of the most radical, racist laws were formulated there, and the state is considered a legislative laboratory for the rest of country: anti-immigrant laws are crafted, promoted, and passed in Arizona first, and then spread out to be taken up by other states.

This is the state where Sheriff Joe Arpaio operated with stunning impunity in Maricopa County, which includes Phoenix, the capital, terrorizing Latino residents in the service of "cleansing" communities of undocumented immigrants. Never mind that those very immigrants tend lawns for everyone else, and build their homes, and take care of their children. Arizona also passed Proposition 200 in 2004, which denied undocumented people access to public services.

SB 1070, passed by the Arizona State Senate on April 19 and signed into law by Governor Brewer four days later, went even further. It not only penalized anyone providing support to an undocumented person, even a family member; it also punished law enforcement officers, in the police and sheriff's department, who failed to detain someone suspected of being undocumented, a practice prohibited by federal law (with rare exceptions).

What is the physical description of an undocumented person? In a country where immigrants come from every corner of the world, and where most immigrants and their descendants have legal immigration status, how do you identify someone as being in the country illegally? For civil rights organizations, the answer was obvious: it would be someone with dark skin, who does not speak English or speaks with an accent, or anyone who speaks Spanish.

Falling under the shadow of suspicion were people who had lived in the region since long before Brigham Young found his way there: people who had brown skin because the hot Arizona sun had darkened their ancestors' complexions for centuries; people with last names like López and Méndez, descended from the Spanish who had first colonized these lands; and people wearing ball caps emblazoned with the Suns logo, their hometown NBA basketball team, or sporting Cardinals jerseys, Arizona's NFL team, documented or not. This was not just an anti-immigrant law. It was racist, placing Arizona in an embarrassing position that in no way reflected the principles of the nation's founding fathers.

By the time Governor Brewer signed SB 1070 into effect, on July 29, 2010, civil and immigrant rights groups had already crafted legal strategies to try to block the law, arguing that no state law can be above the US Constitution and federal laws that prohibit racial profiling. Some of these legal challenges proceeded in court, and the components of the law that encouraged racial profiling were eliminated—at least on paper, although in practice profiling still occurred. Not successfully thrown out completely were the prerogative to deny access to some services to undocumented people and sanctions against employers who hire undocumented workers, which are significant and rigorously applied.

Meanwhile, just a few days after SB 1070 was signed in April, a group of activists, including Luis and Daniel, put out the call to boycott the state of Arizona: do not spend your money there; do not plan any trips there. The idea of a boycott against a whole state may have seemed ludicrous, but the concept had a precedent, and a successful one at that.

In 1983, the third Monday of every January was declared a national holiday to honor civil rights leader Dr. Martin Luther King Jr. But the Arizona state government refused to pass a law that would designate the day a holiday on the state level. In response, in the early 1990s, the Reverend Jesse Jackson, a Baptist minister, human rights activist, and leader in the African American community, organized a boycott against the state that garnered wide support across the country. In 1991, bowing to pressure from many of its African American players, the NFL moved the location of the 1993 Super Bowl from Phoenix to Pasadena, California. The following year, Arizona passed the law.

With that precedent in mind, in response to SB 1070, activist organizations in Arizona called on the Latino community to start a boycott. Leaders urged people to stop attending the games of Arizona sports teams, no matter where they were playing, and asked popular Latino performers to cancel upcoming concerts in the state. They told everyone to stop using US Airways, headquartered in Phoenix, and asked residents of Sonora, Mexico, to stop crossing the border into Arizona to shop. Boycott organizers asked major corporations and business groups to cancel conventions and meetings to be held in Arizona, and they asked the whole country to stop purchasing agricultural products grown in Arizona. Truckers from the Port of Los Angeles, the most important commercial port in the country, pledged to stop transporting shipping containers to Arizona.

The boycott threatened to ostracize some of the state's key industry sectors. Arizona lost thousands of hotel reservations, and major musical acts, such as Manu Chao, Rage Against the Machine, Cypress Hill, and Kanye West, came out in support of the boycott with what they dubbed "The Sound Strike." Other artists, such as Lady Gaga, did not cancel their shows, but they did make public statements condemning SB 1070. All of these actions caught the media's attention; coverage went viral, and the boycott dealt a crippling blow to Arizona tourism, to the tune of $140 million.[1]

Even more important, the passage of SB 1070 sparked an outpouring of criticism against the state in the national public discourse, which in turn inspired organizations, businesses, and thought leaders in other states to sign on to the boycott. The convention industry was the first to be affected when groups and associations started canceling upcoming events in the state. The meetings and conferences that were canceled over the next three years would have helped sustain 2,800 employees, and the economic losses surpassed $86 million in lost wages, plus $250 million in overall lost revenue.[2]

The Arizona Lodging & Hotel Association reported a loss of $15 million in just the four months right after the law was passed, while the Center for American Progress think tank concluded that amount would have been triple, at $45 million. Between July and

August 2010, when the law went into effect, the state's Convention and Visitors Bureau received 35 percent fewer reservations than in the same period the previous year.

Estimates calculated at the time also found the state would have lost revenue from taxes, as well as lost salaries, from the goods and services that workers would have purchased with that lost income, totaling approximately $9 million in two or three years. The *Arizona Republic* figured total losses were $600 million.

Los Angeles; Austin, Texas; and St. Paul, Minnesota, among other city governments, passed measures officially boycotting Arizona, and dozens more made public statements calling for the repeal of SB 1070. In that climate, the Mexican Consulate issued a travel alert warning Mexican citizens that in Arizona they were at risk of being questioned by police for no apparent reason.

The general outcry and social pressure were reflected in the various lawsuits challenging the law, which succeeded in overturning its most draconian aspects. Some parts of the law remain in effect. Though the young activists had not won the war, they did win the battle to minimize the damage.

When Luis and Daniel got together to brainstorm the response to the Trump administration—which ended up being the Mexican boycott of US corn—statements from a former president of Mexico, along with the lessons learned from the Arizona boycott, gave them an indication of what path to take. Luis had just seen former president Felipe Calderón on television, whose administration had maintained a bumpy relationship with the United States because of the "war on drugs" and its effects on bilateral relations. In an interview, Calderón suggested that Mexico stop buying agricultural products such as corn and soy from their neighbor to the north.

Luis told Daniel about it, and Daniel thought that, aside from being a symbolic act, it could actually have a strong impact, without punishing consumers. Some days before, a general boycott of all US products had been initiated in Mexico, which was in practical terms very hard to pull off, not only because of the huge range of US goods that are regularly consumed in Mexico—and the difficulty in identifying them—but also because that would mean boycotting small Mexican business owners who had invested their own money in US products and created jobs for other Mexicans.

"It had to be something really easy for the consumer, and we remembered the boycott that Cesar Chavez had organized," Luis explained to me. "The message was very clear: 'Don't eat grapes,' and that's it. In considering this, we remembered how Cesar Chavez had even gone to Europe to tell them [to] 'stop buying California grapes.' It was very simple, and that was more or less what we did in 2010. The boycott was 'Don't do business in the state of Arizona.' That was very easy, because it didn't imply any big changes in the lives of average Arizonans."

To Luis, corn also had a powerful symbolism. As soon as he and Daniel started talking about the idea with others, a group of young Mexicans decided to support it by making a video with a pointed message: we used to export it, now we import it; migrants headed north, and now we buy corn.

As Luis and Daniel started talking to more people, they realized they were touching on a tremendously relevant issue, which for whatever reason was not on the national public agenda in Mexico. "Before, the only thing we knew about corn was that it's used to make tortillas," Daniel said, only half joking. "Now we know a lot more. Almost 5 percent of all the corn grown in the US is exported to Mexico. That might not sound like much, but that's almost 70 percent of total corn consumption in Mexico, worth billions of dollars. But it's not *nixtamalizado* corn [the type used to make tortillas], which is what people eat; it's yellow corn, which is used for animal feed and in oils and high-fructose corn syrup in sodas. Ninety-nine percent of yellow corn [bought] in Mexico is from the US, and it's used in states that raise a lot of livestock."

A boycott of US corn would deal a strong blow to that country's economy, but it would also put pressure on Mexican industries that depend on that corn, because they would need to find another source. Luis and Daniel believe there's a challenge as well as an opportunity there, and they wanted to promote their idea on the other side of the border: people well-versed in the subject could advise them on what was practical, and what wasn't, and let them know what Mexico was doing in that area.

When they started talking about the concept using social media and contacting organizations in Mexico, people in that country reacted positively, but Luis and Daniel also learned something important: Mexicans do not trust their government. In the current political climate, there would be no shortage of politicians who would want to take up the cause and stamp it with their own political party or issue. How could Luis and Daniel move forward with this kind of initiative without being used, considering both of them were unfamiliar with the political context since they didn't live there?

Almost as soon as they had been warned about the risk of their initiative being exploited by politicians for their own ends, it happened. Just a few days after they began preparing to promote the boycott, starting to build a website and an online petition, Luis and Daniel found out that a delegation of Mexican senators was planning a visit to Arizona. They decided to attend a meeting the senators were having; it was private but Luis and Daniel managed to gain access as journalists along with other representatives of the media. At one point, Luis received permission to speak, and he asked for the Senate delegation's support for the corn boycott. The idea intrigued a staffer working for Armando Ríos Píter, a senator and member of the Democratic Revolutionary Party (PRD). The senator decided to "support" the boycott in his own way. He talked to the press about it, and soon a legislative initiative that he himself signed, based on Luis and Daniel's concept, was ready to be presented in the Mexican Senate.[3]

"That got us coverage; it helped get the word out. The most important publications covering trade treaties and media like National Public Radio and *USA Today* have talked about it, but it's all been focused on the legislative initiative," Luis says, somewhat resigned to having their idea co-opted. "So now what we're trying to do is say, 'Hey, this was our idea, a couple of concerned immigrants,' because if it's just a proposal from the Mexican Senate, then it's like we didn't do anything."

What happened with the Mexican Senate will no doubt serve as one more learning experience for the two young activists, who are still forging ahead. Luis believes a singular moment in time has arrived, a unique set of circumstances that has sparked a renewed, revitalized feeling of national pride in many Mexicans, and they need to take advantage of it.

"It's been amazing for me to see this 'Yes we can' attitude, for the first time, doubting the relationship with the United States," Luis explains enthusiastically. "It's a really interesting reaction, and I believe it's a unique opportunity for whatever renegotiation might take place now. Another thing that has excited me from the beginning is, I think this is the first time Mexicans in Mexico and in the US can do something together, for a common cause."

Another aspect of the Mexican boycott of American corn that particularly excites them is the chance to "speak for others," Daniel explains. They believe that the Trump administration has drawn heightened attention to the US trade agreements, and in the context of a renegotiation, the migration issue will have to be factored into any new versions the agreements. Mexico also has an opportunity to expand its influence: if Mexico starts working with other countries to build a united Latin American leadership, it could change the balance of power with the United States over the long term.

"The United States liked having an economically globalized world. It was very good for the country," Daniel says, adjusting his glasses. He speaks passionately. It is clear that he believes this part of the argument has implications beyond one hostile president's four-year term. "This is the first campaign that I'm aware of that is using the same strategy to politically pressure a government action inside the same country. Are we living in a globalized world? Well, we can use Mexico's influence, which for whatever reason they have not used before, to build social movements. We're starting to educate ourselves about how we can start to exercise that power."

"This isn't just about the Trump administration," Luis adds. "If agreements are broken, if he insults Mexicans, if he damages the relations with Mexico, what happens after Trump? Are we going to be doormats again?"

The months after the "hijacking" of their idea by players in Mexico's political game have given Luis and Daniel the chance to learn what people think about that game. Through social media, especially the boycott campaign's Facebook page, Luis and Daniel receive messages of support from some people who see the boycott as a symbolic condemnation of President Peña Nieto's administration. They hear from others who are suspicious of the motives behind the boycott and accuse Luis and Daniel of being pawns of the government; these posters don't want to add their names in support because they fear that information could be used for other aims. Some have accused Luis and Daniel of creating a "distraction" to divert attention from criticisms of the Mexican government.

"We have been very careful in our response, and we're not moving away from this subject, because we've learned that's what dilutes movements," Luis explains. "We have focused on the idea that this is a unique moment, and we can renegotiate things from a position of strength. And people tell us things. They post on Facebook that they get paid a miserable price for corn; they know the price in the market is higher, but they have no way to transport it. There are Mexican growers who could be good allies. There's a bridge, but we don't know how to cross it. And we have a profile of the people who left Mexico because they lost their land. Between nationalist sentiment and anti-Trumpism, a large part of the campaign's purpose—to examine migration in terms of rural farming areas and NAFTA—gets lost. And that's what we have to focus on now."

Luis and Daniel also see challenges on the US side. One is how to generate interest and awareness among people in the US who are not directly affected by the migration issue. How do you explain to them that what might happen will impact them too? In their research, Daniel and Luis discovered that, with the exception of Illinois, the states with the highest corn-production rates voted Republican. In the 2016 presidential election, Iowa—the greatest corn producer, with 18 percent of total national production—Minnesota, Nebraska, and Kansas all voted for Trump.

Luis and Daniel are plotting the next steps in the corn boycott. Luis told me that in the coming months they will be building alliances in Mexico to continue the conversation independent of the political party that presented the legislative initiative, and they plan to partner with organizations and groups that can take an integrated approach to make the boycott a reality.

"We have to let this develop in Mexico and from there talk about what has to be done, because it's just a question of deciding we're not going to buy anymore," Luis says. "Is there infrastructure to increase corn production in Mexico? On Facebook some people tell us: 'I live in an area where there used to be a lot of land for growing crops, but they've given it to industrial parks.' We can't have these conversations from Phoenix. We have to find allies in Mexico to keep the conversation going and decide what we should do. Should we keep the pressure on in Mexico, or should we focus on the repercussions this could have in the US and turn up the heat on this side?"

We'll see what happens in the next four years, and beyond.

EPILOGUE

DONALD TRUMP, who ran for president boasting of his tremendous skills as a negotiator, vowing that he would "drain the swamp" and manage the government just like a successful business, if elected, finished up his first year in the White House with a government shutdown. And the reason for the collapse was his trademark issue: immigration.

Leading up to the passage of the budget for the administration's second fiscal year, President Trump proposed a deal: Congress would have to approve more money for US-Mexico border security and, in exchange, the government would continue to shield eight hundred thousand Dreamers protected by DACA from deportation. Millions of dollars for border control traded for ongoing stability in undocumented young people's lives.

Immigration as an issue, which was the dominant theme in Trump's campaign rhetoric and in large measure helped propel him to the presidency, continued to play a central role in the narrative of his administration's first year. If his campaign was a jumble of isolationist, xenophobic slogans and promises—build a wall, renegotiate NAFTA, expel certain migrants—there has been a constant effort during his administration to keep people who come from what he described as "shithole countries" on the margins.

In office for less than one hundred days, Trump tried to impose a travel ban on citizens from seven majority-Muslim countries, known as the "Muslim ban." Over the course of the next two hundred days, he announced that Temporary Protected Status (TPS) for Haitians, Nicaraguans, and Salvadorans would not be renewed, and he threatened to withhold federal funds from cities that had declared themselves to be "sanctuaries" for immigrants. And throughout the entire first year, he continuously threatened protections for Dreamers, his favorite bargaining chip. Governmental paralysis marking Trump's first year in office followed the negativity of the congressional majority to approve additional funds for ICE and Border Control. Nevertheless, with most of his proposals related to immigration, Trump's wishes have come up against the reality of a country where, in spite of its many flaws, the rule of law prevails.

The first year of the Trump administration tested the separation of powers in the United States like never before, and so far the country has passed the test. The "Muslim ban" was blocked by various federal judges, and Trump's attempt to rescind DACA was also blocked temporarily by at least two courts. Federal funds destined for "sanctuary cities" have not been withheld, since Congress has not taken up any measure to cut them off. Congress has also put the brakes on plans to hire 15,000 additional ICE agents. And though Trump ordered four prototypes of designs for a border wall, there is no line item anywhere for a wall in the federal budget for his administration's second year.

In spite of this, Trump's rhetoric is powerful. Thousands of media outlets around the world allot ample space and time for covering and amplifying the harsh, crude, heartless expressions of this president, who has found in immigration the perfect distraction from his administration's bigger problems, like the investigation into Russia's interference in the presidential election, the dizzying rate of White House staff turnover, and federal government jobs left long vacant. And although the budget does not allow for hiring more immigration judges, and because of that the number of deportations has not increased, the number of immigration arrests has gone up, stoking a growing feeling of terror among some immigrant communities.[1]

The stories told in this book are an example of how, in the face of this relentless attack, waged with words and media coverage more than actions, Mexican immigrants in the United States are able to organize, regroup, and continue building a life of opportunity and success for themselves and their families. During this administration's first year, Odilia Romero participated in the Food Book Fair to talk about food-industry workers' rights. Mafalda Gueta, now a green-card holder, was able to travel for the first time to Guadalajara, Mexico, her birthplace, to meet her parents' family. Claudia Amaro was given a new court date for her political asylum case in 2021; in the meantime, she can remain in the country with her family. Jeanette Vizguerra had speaking engagements at several universities, where she talked about immigrants' rights. Ana Elena Soto's annual education conference for Latina families raised its attendance to seventeen from seven. Individually, and as a community, immigrants in the United States continue to resist and continue to write their own success stories.

As of this writing, there are still over two years to go in Donald Trump's presidency—or at least the first term. But the 2018 midterm elections offer the perfect juncture for the pro-immigrant movement to become a political actor in the US and, in alliance with other activist movements, to force a change and bring into Congress representatives who are sensitive and empathetic to minority communities.

The Trump era has exposed more clearly than ever the vulnerability of migrants, and as a result, it has made the pro-immigrant movement more relevant. In order to make that relevance more effective, organizations working for the rights of immigrants must recalibrate the strategies they have created in the past and form new alliances that will help broaden the reach of their message.

As the youngest segment of the pro-immigrant movement, the Dreamers set a good example for older, more established organizations working on this issue. With a dialogue that extends beyond an immigration agenda, and thanks to a political maturity developed by trial and error, these young people have built national networks with ethnic, racial, and religious representation. They have created and nurtured intersections with other communities, like the LGBT community—giving rise to the term "undocuqueers"—or the undocumented black community—the "undocublack" movement—and sometimes joined with other mass protest movements like #MeToo

and Black Lives Matter. Although the great majority of Dreamers are Mexican, they have assumed their place in US society in
a broader sense, transcending their status as immigrants. That
is what differentiates Dreamers from the overall pro-immigrant
movement, and it has worked to their advantage.

Over the past twenty years, the groups representing immigrants and driving the immigration agenda forward have gained
a higher level of visibility in the media and a larger presence in
Washington, DC. The Latino vote grew by almost 50 percent between 2004 and 2012, and voter election materials produced in
languages other than English are now distributed in areas that
encompass 68 million voters, or over 40 percent of eligible voters,
but that has not been enough to enact any new measures that
would grant immigrants legal status.[2] The pro-immigrant movement has won some victories at the state and local level to block
measures that amounted to persecution, but it has also suffered
reversals, like the nonrenewal of the TPS program for immigrants
from certain countries.

For Mexican immigrants, Trump is no longer the question mark
he was a year ago. His first months in the White House demonstrated that not only are immigrants' rights in peril in the United
States; civil rights are also threatened. The most recent Human
Rights Watch annual report concludes that while the current administration's policies have affected refugees and immigrants, they
have also resulted in an erosion of women's rights, LGBT rights,
freedom of expression, and accountability.[3]

Veterans of the pro-immigrant movement, who are mostly of
Mexican and Central American origin, would be wise to follow
the example set by the Dreamers, who have learned how to forge
alliances with other sectors of society, sharing information and
creating joint strategies. As a result, over 70 percent of US citizens now support some form of legalization for these young people. Formulating strategies to educate and enlighten communities
who have not traditionally fought for immigrants' rights, but who
have the ability to lobby and exert political influence, could be a
good start. By complementing those efforts with outreach to local

networks that community leaders in some states have nurtured, the overall result could tip the balance in favor of the immigrant community. Organizing events in California, a Democratic-leaning, pro-immigrant state, could boost visibility, but it would not grow the political base. Sending a message to moderates who are willing to listen, in battleground districts where election results could produce a real change, is critical. We must ensure that immigrant voices, telling their stories of strength, triumph, and resistance, reach their ears. After all, that is the true spirit of the United States of America.

ACKNOWLEDGMENTS

JOURNALISTS HAVE A SAYING: every reporter needs a little luck. I think this is true, and for me, my greatest stroke of luck has been having people around me who share my drive to tell stories that matter, the stories happening all around us in real life every day, that can help us understand who we are and how we can be better—as people and as a country. This book comes out of that.

Thanks to Daniel Mesino and Karina Macías at Editorial Planeta for coming up with the idea for this project, which was originally published in Spanish in 2017, and for their faith in me to write it, and to Tania Cabrera for editing the stories of our Mexicans in the North with such sensitivity.

How Does It Feel to Be Unwanted? crossed the border and has been published in English thanks to the steadfast determination of my literary agent, Diane Stockwell, who also performed the excellent translation. To Gayatri Patnaik, thank you for so lovingly shepherding these stories. To Helene Atwan, Susan Lumenello, Molly Velazquez-Brown, Caitlin Meyer, Alyssa Hassan, Sanj Kharbanda, and the entire team at Beacon Press, I am grateful for your trust and support.

This project was planned and executed in six months. I could not have written it without the support of the Faber Residency, an arts and humanities retreat in Olot, Catalonia, in Spain, where most of this book took shape. I am grateful to the director Francesc Serés for the space and for his faith and empathy.

Most of the stories in this book are continuations of subjects I have been writing about for the past fourteen years. I am extremely grateful to the editors I have worked with over the course of that time: Salvador Frausto, Gabriel Lerner, Karla Casillas, Guillermo Osorno, Andrés Tapia, Homero Campa, Ernesto Núñez, Elizabeth Palacios, and the dearly missed José Luis Sierra.

Thanks so much to those who helped me revise and edit the manuscript, against the clock: Diego Sedano, Catalina Gayá, Armando Vega-Gil, Alaíde Ventura, Sofía Téllez, and Toni Piqué.

Reporters are only as good as the journalism family who raises them, and I am still learning from mine every day. Thanks to Salvador Frausto, Témoris Grecko, Catalina Gayá, and the members of our collective, Cuadernos Doble Raya. To Diego Fonseca, Wilbert Torre, José Luis Benavides, and Antonio Mejías-Rentas, for their always welcome advice. As always, I am grateful to my family of seven years at *La Opinión*, the daily newspaper that opened the doors to many of these stories.

Without the generosity of its protagonists, there can be no story. From the bottom of my heart, thanks to Omar León; Claudia Amaro; Yamil Yáujar; Yunuen Bonaparte; Alberto Mendoza; Jennicet Gutiérrez; Mónica Robles; Odilia Romero; Jeanette Vizguerra; Al Labrada; Noemí, Cynthia, and María Romero; Viridiana Hernández; Mafalda and Carlos Gueta; Ana Elena Soto; Daniel Rodríguez; and Luis Ávila for sharing their stories of triumph and resistance.

This book unfolded during a very turbulent time. Thanks to Eliesheva Ramos and my sister Rosal for staying close. To Diego Sedano and to my mother, I cannot thank you enough for your constancy, support, and love.

NOTES

INTRODUCTION
    1. Southern Poverty Law Center, "Hate Groups 1999–2017," https://www
.splcenter.org/hate-map.
    2. FBI, "2012 Hate Crime Statistics," https://ucr.fbi.gov/hate-crime/2012.

CHAPTER ONE: A BETTER LIFE
    1. David Bacon, "Living Under the Trees: Indigenous Mexican Farm Workers
in California," *Beacon Broadside* (blog of Beacon Press), May 6, 2008, http://
www.beaconbroadside.com/broadside/2008/05/living-under-th.html.
    2. Abel Valenzuela Jr., Nik Theodore, Edwin Meléndez, and Ana Luz Gonza-
lez, *On the Corner: Day Labor in the United States* (Los Angeles: Center for the
Study of Urban Poverty, UCLA, January 2006), http://portlandvoz.org/wp-content
/uploads/images/2009/04/national-study.pdf.
    3. Alto Trump!, "Stand Up Against Hatred, Bigotry and Xenophobia," No-
vember 11, 2016, http://altotrump.com.

CHAPTER TWO: WHY DON'T THEY WANT US?
    1. Agence France-Presse, "Trump Win Breathes Life into the Private Prison
Industry," *Raw Story*, November 25, 2016, http://www.rawstory.com/2016/11
/trump-win-breathes-life-into-the-private-prison-industry.
    2. Office of the Inspector General, US Department of Justice, *Review of the
Federal Bureau of Prisons' Monitoring of Contract Prisons* (Washington, DC: US
Department of Justice, August 2016).
    3. Paul Blumenthal, "Private Prison Company Backs Super PACs for Trump,
Senate Republicans," *Huffington Post Mexico*, October 24, 2016, http://www
.huffingtonpost.com.mx/entry/donald-trump-private-prison_us_580e7b02e4
b000d0b1583000.
    4. Department of Homeland Security, *Yearbook of Immigration Statistics*
(Washington, DC: DHS, November 14, 2017), https://www.dhs.gov/immigration
-statistics/yearbook; Muzaffar Chishti, Sarah Pierce, and Jessica Bolte, "The
Obama Record on Deportations: Deporter in Chief or Not?," Migrationpolicy
.org. March 22, 2017, https://www.migrationpolicy.org/article/obama-record
-deportations-deporter-chief-or-not.
    5. Transactional Records Access Clearinghouse (TRAC), *Secure Communi-
ties and ICE Deportation: A Failed Program?* (April 8, 2014), http://trac.syr
.edu/immigration/reports/349.

6. Randy Capps, Sarah Hooker, Heather Koball, Juan Manuel Pedroza, Andrea Campetella, and Krista Perreira, "Implications of Immigration Enforcement Activities for the Well-Being of Children in Immigrant Families," September 2015, Urban Institute and Migration Policy Institute, https://www.urban.org /sites/default/files/alfresco/publication-exhibits/2000405/2000405-Implications -of-Immigration-Enforcement-Activities-for-the-Well-Being-of-Children-in -Immigrant-Families.pdf.

7. Department of Homeland Security, *Yearbook of Immigration Statistics*, https://www.dhs.gov/immigration-statistics/yearbook/2016/table39.

CHAPTER THREE: OAXACALIFORNIA

1. "Quiénes somos," Frente Indígena de Organizaciones Binacionales (FIOB), http://fiob.org/quienes-somos, accessed January 9, 2018.

2. National Institute of Statistics and Geography, Instituto Nacional de Estadística y Geografía (INEGI), Mexico, Census, 2010 (in Spanish), http://www .beta.inegi.org.mx/temas/lengua/default.html.

3. Instituto Nacional de las Mujeres et al., *Las mujeres indígenas de México: Su contexto socioeconómico, demográphico y de salud* (Indigenous women in Mexico: social, economic, demographic, and health context), October 2006, 21, http://cedoc.inmujeres.gob.mx/documentos_download/100833.pdf.

4. Ibid.

5. L. Miranda, "Pierde a su hija por no hablar español ni inglés," *El Oaxaqueño*, August 28, 2009.

6. FIOB, Programa de los Intérpretes Indígenas, "Intérpretes Indígenas: Puente Imprescindible Entre Culturas," http://centrobinacional.org/programas /fresno/programa-de-los-interpretes-indigenas.

7. Children's Hospital Los Angeles, "History," November 16, 2016, accessed January 9, 2018, http://www.chla.org/history.

8. Eileen Truax, "¿Cómo se dice 'censo' en zapoteco?," *La Opinión*, January 9, 2010.

CHAPTER FOUR: A QUESTION OF HONOR

1. Centers for Disease Control and Prevention, "HIV Among Hispanics/ Latinos," September 26, 2017, https://www.cdc.gov/hiv/group/racialethnic /hispaniclatinos/index.html.

2. Euronews video, "'You're in My House,' Obama Shuts Down a Heckler During Speech," June 25, 2014, https://youtu.be/HpF9ObMoIDc.

3. Eileen Truax, "La transgénero que incomodó a Obama," *El Universal*, July 5, 2015, http://www.eluniversal.com.mx/articulo/periodismo-de-investigacion /2015/07/5/la-transgenero-que-incomodo-obama.

4. Cristina Costantini, Jorge Rivas, and Kristofer Ríos, *Why Did the U.S. Lock Up These Women with Men?*, Fusion Special Report, November 17, 2014, http://interactive.fusion.net/trans.

5. Quote from video posted on NDLON website.

6. Mitch Kellaway and Sunnivie Brydum, "The 21 Trans Women Killed in 2015," *Advocate*, July 27, 2015, https://www.advocate.com/transgender/2015/07 /27/these-are-trans-women-killed-so-far-us-2015.

7. "These Are the Trans People Killed in 2016," Advocate.com, https://www
.advocate.com/transgender/2016/10/14/these-are-trans-people-killed-2016.

8. "Who We Are," Honor 41, http://honor41.org, accessed January 9, 2018.

CHAPTER FIVE: SANCTUARY

1. I re-created the scene of Jeanette Vizguerra's arrival at the sanctuary based
on my conversation with her on May 25, 2017; the CNN story by Donie O'Sullivan and Sara Weisfeldt, http://edition.cnn.com/2017/04/20/us/vizguerra-time-100
-trnd/index.html; and Sarah Pulliam Bailey, "This Undocumented Immigrant Just
Announced That She Is Seeking Sanctuary at a Church. Now She Waits," *Washington Post*, February 15, 2017, https://www.washingtonpost.com/news/acts-of
-faith/wp/2017/02/15/this-undocumented-immigrant-just-announced-shes-seeking
-sanctuary-at-a-church-now-she-waits.

2. F. James Sensenbrenner Jr., "H.R.4437—109th Congress (2005–2006):
Border Protection, Antiterrorism, and Illegal Immigration Control Act of 2005,"
Congress.gov, January 27, 2006, https://www.congress.gov/bill/109th-congress
/house-bill/4437.

3. US Immigration and Customs Enforcement, John Morton memo re
"Secretary Napolitano's Memorandum Concerning the Exercise of Prosecutorial
Discretion for Certain Removable Individuals Who Entered the United States as a
Child," https://www.ice.gov/doclib/about/offices/ero/pdf/s1-certain-young-people
-morton.pdf.

4. US Immigration and Customs Enforcement, "FY 2016 ICE Immigration
Removals," https://www.ice.gov/removal-statistics/2016, accessed January 9,
2017.

5. Bryan Baker and Christopher Williams, "Immigration Enforcement Actions: 2014," Department of Homeland Security, January 2016, https://www.dhs
.gov/sites/default/files/publications/Enforcement_Actions_2014.pdf.

6. According to Rev. Noel Anderson from the World Church movement in an
interview with the *Washington Post*. Rev. Anderson has followed the Sanctuary
movement for many years. Bailey, "This Undocumented Immigrant Just Announced That She Is Seeking Sanctuary at a Church. Now She Waits."

7. "Criminal Justice Fact Sheet," NAACP, 2015, http://www.naacp.org
/criminal-justice-fact-sheet; Sophia Kerby, "The Top 10 Most Startling Facts
About People of Color and Criminal Justice in the United States," Center for
American Progress, March 13, 2012, https://www.americanprogress.org/issues
/race/news/2012/03/13/11351/the-top-10-most-startling-facts-about-people-of
-color-and-criminal-justice-in-the-united-states.

8. CNN, "Black vs. White Man Breaking into Car," 2014, https://www.cnn
.com/videos/bestoftv/2014/02/23/nr-car-prank-racism-long.cnn.

9. Darla Cameron, "How Sanctuary Cities Work, and How Trump's Blocked
Executive Order Could Have Affected Them," *Washington Post*, January 18,
2017, https://www.washingtonpost.com/graphics/national/sanctuary-cities.

10. "Women's Refugee Commission Announces Support for We Belong
Together Kids Caravan and Week of Action," April 10, 2017, Women's Refugee
Commission, https://www.womensrefugeecommission.org/news/press-releases
-and-statements/2596-wrc-support-we-belong-together-kids-caravan.

11. "Sanctuary Everywhere," American Friends Service Committee, https://www.afsc.org/sanctuaryeverywhere, accessed January 9, 2018.

12. America Ferrera, "Jeanette Vizguerra," The 100 Most Influential People, *Time*, 2017, http://time.com/collection/2017-time-100/4736271/jeanette-vizguerra.

CHAPTER SIX: A LIFE LIVED WITHIN TWENTY-NINE MILES

1. Travis Mitchell, "U.S. Unauthorized Immigration Population Estimates," November 3, 2016, Pew Research Center, Hispanic Trends project, http://www.pewhispanic.org/interactives/unauthorized-immigrants.

2. Anat Bracha and Mary A. Burke, "Informal Work in the United States: Evidence from Survey Responses," Federal Reserve Bank of Boston, March 31, 2014, https://www.bostonfed.org/publications/current-policy-perspectives/2014/informal-work-in-the-united-states-evidence-from-survey-responses.aspx; US Customs and Border Protection, "Border Patrol Sectors," https://www.cbp.gov/border-security/along-us-borders/border-patrol-sectors, accessed January 9, 2018.

3. As of March 2018, the budget approved by Congress has not included resources to hire these new Border Patrol agents. During the budget discussion in the Senate in January 2018, this was one of the conditions that the Republican Party asked to be included in exchange for some kind of legislation to protect the undocumented youth known as Dreamers.

4. US Customs and Border Protection, "Border Patrol Sectors."

5. Bob Ortega, "Interior Border Checks Spur Suit," *Arizona Republic*, January 16, 2014, http://archive.azcentral.com/news/politics/articles/20140115interior-border-checks-spur-suit.html.

6. "ACLU Factsheet on the Constitution in the 100-Mile Zone," American Civil Liberties Union, https://www.aclu.org/other/constitution-100-mile-border-zone.

7. Manny Fernandez, "Checkpoints Isolate Many Immigrants in Texas' Rio Grande Valley," *New York Times*, November 22, 2015, https://www.nytimes.com/2015/11/23/us/checkpoints-isolate-many-immigrants-in-texas-rio-grande-valley.html.

8. Kevin Johnson, "The Arizona Lawman Challenging President Trump's Border Wall," *USA Today*, March 5, 2017, https://www.usatoday.com/story/news/2017/03/05/arizona-lawman-challenging-president-trumps-border-wall/98492128.

9. *Texas Border Business*, "Texas Mayors United Asking Congress to Oppose 'Reckless Policies' Regarding Our U.S. Border and Mexico, Our Neighbor and Trading Partner," February 3, 2017, https://texasborderbusiness.com/texas-mayors-united-asking-congress-oppose-reckless-policies-regarding-u-s-border-mexico-neighbor-trading-partner.

CHAPTER SEVEN: LIFE IS NO DISNEYLAND

1. *PBS NewsHour*, "Watch Hillary Clinton Answer Questions at 2016 NABJ/NAHJ Joint Convention," YouTube video, August 5, 2016, https://www.youtube.com/watch?v=qoB-gOZY5OM.

2. Lindsey Graham, "S.1615—115th Congress (2017–2018): Dream Act of 2017," Congress.gov, July 20, 2017, https://www.congress.gov/bill/115th-congress/senate-bill/1615.

3. US Immigration and Customs Enforcement, "FY 2016 ICE Immigration Removals," December 5, 2017, https://www.ice.gov/removal-statistics/2016#_ftnref3.

4. College Board, Trends in Higher Education, "Average Published Undergraduate Charges by Sector and by Carnegie Classification, 2017–18," https://trends.collegeboard.org/college-pricing/figures-tables/average-published-undergraduate-charges-sector-2016-17.

5. US Citizenship and Immigration Services, "DHS Outlines Deferred Action for Childhood Arrivals Process," August 3, 2012, https://www.uscis.gov/news/dhs-outlines-deferred-action-childhood-arrivals-process. DACA was announced during Obama's reelection campaign in 2012 and was seen as a means to pressure Congress to pass the immigration reform legislation presented in 2013, at the beginning of his second term. But DACA was also the result of years of intensive lobbying, protesting, and organizing by the Dreamers themselves, at the local and national level. See Eileen Truax, *Dreamers: An Immigrant Generation's Fight for Their American Dream* (Boston: Beacon Press, 2013).

6. Jens Manuel Krogstad, "DACA Has Shielded Nearly 790,000 Young Unauthorized Immigrants from Deportation," Pew Research Center, September 1, 2017, http://www.pewresearch.org/fact-tank/2017/09/01/unauthorized-immigrants-covered-by-daca-face-uncertain-future.

7. Tom K. Wong et al., "New Study of DACA Beneficiaries Shows Positive Economic and Educational Outcomes," October 18, 2016, Center for American Progress, https://www.americanprogress.org/issues/immigration/news/2016/10/18/146290/new-study-of-daca-beneficiaries-shows-positive-economic-and-educational-outcomes.

8. Michael D. Shear and Julie Hirschfeld Davis, "Trump Moves to End DACA and Calls on Congress to Act," *New York Times*, September 5, 2017, https://www.nytimes.com/2017/09/05/us/politics/trump-daca-dreamers-immigration.html.

CHAPTER EIGHT: CAPTAIN OF HIS PEOPLE
1. Kim Parker, Anthony Cilluffo, and Renee Stepler, "6 Facts About the US Military and Its Changing Demographics," Pew Research Center, April 13, 2017, http://www.pewresearch.org/fact-tank/2017/04/13/6-facts-about-the-u-s-military-and-its-changing-demographics.

2. Jens Manuel Krogstad, "5 Facts About Latinos and Education," Pew Research Center, July 28, 2016, http://www.pewresearch.org/fact-tank/2016/07/28/5-facts-about-latinos-and-education.

3. Amy Navvab, "Cultural Competency Key to Meeting the Health Needs of Latino Veterans," Center for American Progress, November 10, 2012, https://www.americanprogress.org/issues/race/news/2012/08/07/12037/cultural-competency-key-to-meeting-the-health-needs-of-latino-veterans.

4. Christine Eith and Matthew R. Durose, "Contacts Between Police and the Public, 2008," US Department of Justice, Bureau of Justice Statistics, October 2011, https://www.bjs.gov/content/pub/pdf/cpp08.pdf.

5. Kenan Davis et al., "The Counted: The Definitive Map of US Police Killings in 2015," *Guardian*, June 1, 2015, https://www.theguardian.com/us-news/ng-interactive/2015/jun/01/the-counted-map-us-police-killings.

6. Gustavo López and Jens Manuel Krogstad, "How Hispanic Police Officers View Their Jobs," Pew Research Center, February 15, 2017, http://www.pew research.org/fact-tank/2017/02/15/how-hispanic-police-officers-view-their-jobs.

7. The survey was conducted by the National Police Research Platform, May 19–August 14, 2016, and collected the views of a nationally representative sample of 7,917 sworn officers working in 54 police and sheriff's departments with 100 or more officers.

8. Eileen Truax, "Soñadores a pesar de Trump," *Revista Cambio*, February 2017, http://www.revistacambio.com.mx/mundo/sonadores-a-pesar-de-trump.

CHAPTER NINE: FAMILIES CAUGHT BETWEEN TWO WORLDS

1. "Unauthorized Immigrants: Length of Residency, Patterns of Parenthood," Pew Research Center, Hispanic Trends project, December 1, 2017, http://www .pewhispanic.org/2011/12/01/unauthorized-immigrants-length-of-residency -patterns-of-parenthood.

2. Randy Capps, Michael Fix, and Jie Zong, "A Profile of US Children with Unauthorized Immigrant Parents," Migration Policy Institute, April 7, 2017, http://www.migrationpolicy.org/research/profile-us-children-unauthorized -immigrant-parents.

3. Guillermo Cantor, "Thousands of US-Citizen Children Separated from Parents, ICE Records Show," American Immigration Council, Immigration Impact project, March 9, 2016, http://immigrationimpact.com/2014/06/26/thousands -of-u-s-citizen-children-separated-from-parents-ice-records-show.

4. My interviews with the Romero family were done with support from the Immigration in the Heartland program of the Institute for Justice and Journalism (IJJ). Excerpts from the interview were published in my *Huffington Post* story, "Dos realidades en una sola familia," November 1, 2013, http://www.huffington post.com/eileen-truax/dos-realidades-una-familia_b_4195095.html.

5. I've followed the story of Viridiana Hernández since 2012, when I first interviewed her while doing the research for my book about Dreamers. The last time I saw her was in February 2017, in Phoenix. By then she had regularized her immigration status and was working for an immigrant rights organization in that city.

6. Gardenia Mendoza, "Lupita García de Rayos abre tortillería en Guanajuato tras deportación," *La Opinión*, June 5, 2017, https://laopinion.com/2017 /06/05/lupita-garcia-de-rayos-abre-tortilleria-en-michoacan-tras-deportacion.

CHAPTER TEN: LITTLE LEGS, BIG DREAMS

1. At the time, Shriners didn't have a hospital in Mexico. They opened one in Mexico City in 2006. More information can be found on their website: https:// www.shrinershospitalsforchildren.org/shc.

2. Eileen Truax, "Vivir con miedo," *Proceso*, June 6, 2015, http://hemeroteca .proceso.com.mx/?page_id=278958&a51dc26366d99bb5fa29cea4747565fec =406683&rl=wh.

3. The five parts of the study's report, *Undocumented and Uninsured*, can be downloaded at https://www.labor.ucla.edu/healthy-california.

4. Emanuella Grinberg, "Protesters, Riot Police Clash over Arizona Immigration Law," CNN.com, July 29, 2010, http://edition.cnn.com/2010/US/07/29 /arizona.immigration.protests.

CHAPTER ELEVEN: THE FUTURE IS FEMALE

1. Patricia Gándara, "Making Education Work for Latinas in the US," June 2, 2014, US Department of Education, White House Initiative on Educational Excellence for Hispanics, https://sites.ed.gov/hispanic-initiative/2014/06/making -education-work-for-latinas-in-the-u-s.

2. "Women Helping Women Reach for the Stars/P.E.O. International," https://www.peointernational.org, accessed January 9, 2018.

3. Patricia Gándara, "Fulfilling America's Future: Latinas in the US, 2015," October 31, 2015, Civil Rights Project and White House Initiative on Educational Excellence for Hispanics, https://sites.ed.gov/hispanic-initiative/files/2015 /09/Fulfilling-Americas-Future-Latinas-in-the-U.S.-2015-Final-Report.pdf; Sarah Catherine K. Moore, Molly Fee, Jongyeon Ee, Terrence G. Wiley, and M. Beatriz Arias, "Exploring Bilingualism, Literacy, Employability and Income Levels Among Latinos in the United States," in *The Bilingual Advantage: Language, Literacy and the US Labor Market,* ed. Rebecca M. Callahan and Patricia C. Gándara (Bristol, UK: Multilingual Matters), 16–44.

4. National Center for Education Statistics, *Higher Education: Gaps in Access and Persistence Study* (Washington, DC: August 2012), http://nces.ed.gov /pubs2012/2012046.pdf.

5. Annie E. Casey Foundation, *KIDS COUNT Data Book* (2014), 19, http:// www.aecf.org/m/resourcedoc/aecf-2014kidscountdatabook-2014.pdf.

6. Gándara, "Fulfilling America's Future."

7. Robert Crosnoe, *Mexican Roots, American Schools: Helping Mexican Immigrant Children Succeed* (Palo Alto, CA: Stanford University Press, 2006).

CHAPTER TWELVE: LAWYER DREAMS

1. Eileen Truax, "EU: El abogado García litiga por su sueño . . . ejercer," *Proceso,* October 4, 2014, http://hemeroteca.proceso.com.mx/?p=354533.

2. "Immigrants in Arizona," American Immigration Council fact sheet, October 26, 2017, https://www.americanimmigrationcouncil.org/research /immigrants-in-arizona; "Demographic and Economic Profiles of Hispanics by State and County, 2014," Pew Research Center, Hispanic Trends project, July 26, 2011, http://www.pewhispanic.org/states/state/az.

CHAPTER THIRTEEN: BOYCOTT

1. Marshall Fitz and Angela Maria Kelley, "Stop the Conference: The Economic and Fiscal Consequences of Conference Cancellations Due to Arizona's S.B. 1070," November 18, 2010, Center for American Progress, https://www .americanprogress.org/issues/immigration/reports/2010/11/18/8657/stop-the -conference.

2. Ibid.

3. Armando Ríos Piter, "Ni maiz, Trump," *Excélsior,* February 27, 2017, http://www.excelsior.com.mx/opinion/armando-rios-piter/2017/02/27/1148893.

EPILOGUE

1. In fact, in the first year of the Trump administration the number of deportations, 226,000, was significantly lower than in 2013, the year of the Obama administration with the most deportations, when there had been 433,000; see

https://www.dhs.gov/immigration-statistics/yearbook/2016/table39 and https://www.ice.gov/sites/default/files/documents/Document/2017/iceByTheNumbers FY17Infographic.pdf; ICE, *Fiscal Year 2017 ICE Enforcement and Removal Operations Report*, https://www.ice.gov/sites/default/files/documents/Report/2017/iceEndOfYearFY2017.pdf.

2. Jens Manuel Krogstad, "Key Facts About the Latino Vote in 2016," Pew Research Center, 2016, http://www.pewresearch.org/fact-tank/2016/10/14/key-facts-about-the-latino-vote-in-2016/; D'Vera Cohn, "More Voters Will Have Access to Non-English Ballots in the Next Election Cycle," Pew Research Center, 2016, http://www.pewresearch.org/fact-tank/2016/12/16/more-voters-will-have-access-to-non-english-ballots-in-the-next-election-cycle/.

3. Human Rights Watch, chapter on the US, *World Report 2018*, https://www.hrw.org/world-report/2018/country-chapters/united-states.